The Meaning of Mind

BOOKS BY THOMAS SZASZ

The Meaning of Mind

Language, Morality, and Neuroscience

THOMAS SZASZ

PRAEGER

Westport, Connecticut
London

Library of Congress Cataloging-in-Publication Data

Szasz, Thomas Stephen.
    The meaning of mind : language, morality, and neuroscience / Thomas
Szasz.
       p. cm.
    Includes bibliographical references and indexes.
    ISBN 0-275-95603-2 (alk. paper)
    1. Philosophy of mind. 2. Language and languages—Philosophy.
3. Ethics. I. Title.
BD418.3.S93 1996
128'.2—dc20   96-2207

British Library Cataloguing in Publication Data is available.

Library of Congress Catalog Card Number: 96-2207
ISBN: 0-275-95603-2

First published in 1996

Praeger Publishers, 88 Post Road West, Westport, CT 06881
An imprint of Greenwood Publishing Group, Inc.

Printed in the United States of America

The paper used in this book complies with the
Permanent Paper Standard issued by the National
Information Standards Organization (Z39.48-1984).

10 9 8 7 6 5 4 3 2 1

FOR STEVE

Contents

Preface

The word "mind" names one of our most important, but most confused and confusing, ideas. The Latin *mens* means not only mind but also intention and will, a signification still present in our use of the word "mind" as a verb. Because we attribute intention only to intelligent, sentient beings, minding implies agency.

My aim in this book is to present a systematic exploration and exposition of the thesis that minding is the ability to pay attention and adapt to one's environment *by using language to communicate with others and oneself*.* Specifically, I suggest that viewing "the mind" as a potentially infinite variety of self-conversations** is the key that unlocks many of the mysteries we associate with this concept. Animals communicate with other members of their species. But only human beings talk to themselves and recognize that that is what they are doing.

The concept of mind—as the attribution of moral agency to some persons but not others—plays a crucial role in moral philosophy.

---

*By language, I here mean spoken or written words in the case of hearing and sighted persons, speech and Braille in the case of blind persons, and sign language in the case of deaf persons.

**Webster's* lists more than five hundred entries for terms with the prefix "self"—beginning with self-abandonment and ending with self-willed—but "self-conversation" is not among them. Conversation between two persons is called a "dialogue," and the monopolizing of a conversation by a single person is called a "monologue." Hence, the proper Latin word for self-conversation is "autologue."

Infants and demented old persons cannot communicate by language and are therefore typically excluded from the category of moral agents. In the past, persons able to communicate by language—for example, slaves and women—were also denied the status of moral agents; today, many children and mental patients—similarly endowed—are denied that status. The point is that attributing or refusing to attribute moral agency to the Other is a matter of both fact and tactic—a decision that depends not only on the Other's abilities, but also on our attitude toward him. To be recognized as a moral agent, an individual must be able and willing to function as a responsible member of society, and society must be willing to ascribe that capacity and status to him.

The dependence of moral agency on mindedness renders the judgment of mindlessness of paramount legal and social significance. Two common tactics—ignored by classic and modern moral philosophers alike—deserve special mention in this connection. One is treating a person as incompetent when in fact he is not (thus harming him under the guise of helping him); the other is treating a person as a victim when in fact he is an active agent (excusing him of responsibility for his self-victimization and blaming his self-injury on innocent third parties).

Although mind is a moral and psychological concept, it is now regularly addressed by biologists, linguists, mathematicians, neuroscientists, philosophers, and physicists as well. Most of these authors ignore the actual uses of the term "mind." Instead, they treat the mind as if it were the brain, or a function of the brain, and define their task as offering observations and speculations about the workings of that organ.* To properly evaluate the merits of these studies we must not lose sight of the fact that the word "mind" is a part of our everyday vocabulary and that we use it most often, with the most far-reaching practical consequences, in ordinary discourse, law, and psychiatry.

---

*Equally unhelpfully, linguists use constructs and terms such as "artificial intelligence," "mental grammar," and "universal grammar" to explain the workings of the mind.

Acknowledgments

I have profited from the advice of family members, friends, and colleagues. I owe special thanks to my brother George and to my daughter and son-in-law, Margot and Steve Peters. Charles Howard, John Huszonek, Dan Klein, Sanford Kline, Lydia Lehmann, David Levy, Robert Schneebeli, and Roger Yanow read the manuscript, some in several versions, and offered helpful criticisms and suggestions.

As always, I have depended on and benefited from the devoted and knowledgeable assistance of Peter Uva, librarian at the SUNY Health Science Center in Syracuse. I will never be able to thank him enough.

The Meaning of Mind

1

Thought: Self-conversation

Today, the word "mind" functions as both noun and verb. It was not always so. Before the sixteenth century—when persons had souls, not minds—the word "mind" meant only minding.

The birth of the concept of mind as an entity and of the noun "mind" as its name is a symptom of the metamorphosis of the medieval, religious view of the world into the modern, scientific view of it. As a noun, the mind resembles its predecessor, the soul, each naming an unobservable entity. Only in its verbal form—as in "never mind" or "minding the baby"—does the word "mind" have an observable meaning.

Because there is no observable entity called the "mind," we identify the concept in terms of certain activities which we attribute to it, foremost among them thinking. This raises the question, What is thinking? Plato answered that it is talking to oneself. In the *Theaetetus*, he wrote:

SOCRATES: . . . And do you accept my description of the process of thinking?

THEAETETUS: How do you describe it?

SOCRATES: As a discourse that the mind* carries on with itself about any subject it is considering. . . . when the mind is thinking, it is simply talking

---

*This, of course, is an English translation of the Greek text and does not imply use of the word "mind" as a noun prior to the sixteenth century. As I show later (chapter 5), the ancient Greeks had no word for "mind."

to itself. . . . So I should describe thinking as discourse, and judgment as a statement pronounced, not aloud to someone else, but silently to oneself.[1]

I believe that recognizing self-conversation as an ordinary, ubiquitous act—not the symptom of an abnormal mental state—is a prerequisite for understanding the various uses and abuses of the word "mind." Although animals and infants are obviously sentient beings, since they lack the capacity to record and recall experience, their existence seems unlikely to transcend the present. The absence of language—and hence of a past and a future—from their lives renders speculations about their minds moot.

MIND AND LANGUAGE

The connection between mind-as-reason and language is indelibly engraved in the etymology of Latin and the languages derived from it. The Latin *ratio* means calculation or reason, and *oratio* means speech and language. If reason is manifested through language, so also is unreason. This correlation alone should be enough to make us question the now fashionable attribution of reason to schooling and self-discipline, and unreason to chemicals causing neurotransmitters to malfunction.

Mind is dependent on language, as respiration is dependent on the lung. However, mind is neither brain, nor self, nor language, but the person's ability to have a conversation with himself—the self acting as both speaker and listener—the "I" and the "me" speaking and listening to one another. When we talk to ourselves while asleep, we are dreaming.* When we talk to ourselves while awake—in ways permitted in our society—we are thinking or praying. And when we talk to ourselves while awake—in ways prohibited in our society—we are (said to be) crazy.

People intuitively recognize that thinking is self-conversation and that talking and listening to oneself is an ordinary, normal phenomenon. For example, when cultural critic Harold Bloom tells *Newsweek* that "The utility of literature is to teach us not how to talk to others, but how to talk to ourselves,"[2] the reader has no

---

*Because inner speech is disinhibited during sleep, in our dreams we "say" and "see" things involuntarily. I shall have more to say about the control of speaking, and not speaking, later.

difficulty understanding what Bloom means. Today, however, this understanding is limited to certain contexts, especially literature and religion. In others—especially where the question of mental health is on the table—people reflexively believe that a person who talks to himself is *ipso facto* crazy. Perhaps for this reason, writers on the mind who aspire to be taken seriously by the intellectual establishment tend to ignore this phenomenon. Only humorists acknowledge its ubiquity and importance. "I like to talk to myself," quips comedian Jackie Mason, "because I like to deal with a better class of people." The shock value of Karl Kraus's famous aphorism—"Intercourse with a woman may be a satisfactory substitute for masturbation, but it requires a lot of imagination to make it work"[3]—rests on a similar tacit recognition of the pervasive role of inner dialogue in everyday life.

The Story of Helen Keller

Many students of the mind believe that "it" develops in tandem with language. This view, with which I agree, is often illustrated and supported by the story of Helen Keller.

Helen Keller was a healthy baby. When she was nineteen months old, she developed meningitis that rendered her blind and deaf, and hence mute as well. Soon, she became an impulsive, uncontrollable, seemingly retarded child. Only the combination of two fortunate circumstances saved her from a dismal life in an institution. One was that her parents were exceptionally devoted, intelligent, and wealthy as well; the other was that they found, in the person of Anne Sullivan, an exceptionally gifted and tender person to love, care for, and teach their severely handicapped daughter. When Sullivan joined the Keller household, Helen was a six-and-a-half year-old "wild creature." Thanks to Sullivan, she grew up to become an accomplished and independent person.

Because she was deaf, Helen did not learn to speak—that is learn language—at the usual age, in the usual way. Instead, she learned language much later, when Anne Sullivan began to "write" in the palm of her hand and taught her to connect the signs she made with familiar objects, such as water flowing from a tap. In her autobiography, Helen recalled the experience:

As the cool stream gushed over one hand she spelled into the other the word *water,* first slowly, then rapidly. I stood still, my whole attention fixed upon the motions of her fingers. Suddenly I felt a misty consciousness as of something forgotten—a thrill of returning thought; and somehow the mystery of language was revealed to me. I knew then that 'w-a-t-e-r' meant the wonderful cool something that was flowing over my hand. That living word awakened my soul, gave it light, joy, set it free.[4]

Within weeks, Helen was miraculously transformed from a seemingly retarded deaf-mute into an inquisitive, intelligent child. She learned to communicate not only by sign language but also by the spoken word. Her speech remained imperfect, but understandable.*

It must be noted here that just as the hearing person's organs of speech are the tongue, larynx, and lungs, the deaf persons's organs of speech are the fingers, hands, and eyes. When a deaf person thinks, he moves his fingers. Three months after arriving in the Keller household, Sullivan reports to Michael Anagnos, director of the Perkins Institute for the Blind in Boston, where she was trained:

The doctor says her mind is too active; but how are we to keep her from thinking? She begins to spell the minute she wakes up in the morning and continues all day long. If I refuse to talk to her, she spells into her own hand, and apparently carries on the liveliest conversation with herself.[5]

Ten days later, Sullivan continues:

We are bothered a good deal by people who assume the responsibility of the world when God is neglectful. They tell us that Helen is "overdoing," that her mind is too active (*these very people thought she had no mind at all a few months ago!*) and suggest many absurd and impossible remedies. But so far nobody seems to have thought of chloroforming her, which is, I think, the only effective way of stopping the natural exercise of her faculties.[6]**

John Albert Macy, the editor of Keller's autobiography, emphasizes that Helen talked to herself through her organs of "speech," her hands: "Miss Keller talks to herself absent-mindedly in the manual alphabet. When she is walking up or down the hall or along the veranda, her hands go flying along beside her like a confusion

*This process of mind-making through language can also be reversed. If brain disease deprives a person of his ability to use language, he soon loses his mind as well. That is what makes senility resemble a return trip to infancy,

**If this were happening today, the child would probably be diagnosed as suffering from Attention Deficit Disorder and given Ritalin.

of birds' wings."[7] Since one cannot hide the movement of one's hands as easily as one can the movements of one's tongue, it is moot whether Helen was talking to herself "aloud" or "silently."

Did Helen Keller think "in" or "with" her hands? Was her mind "in" her hands? Such questions help us appreciate our need for the concept of mind as well as the confusions it creates. When two persons talk to one another, their conversation occurs in the physical space they occupy or over an electronic connection. By analogy, we might say that a person's self-conversation occurs in the metaphorical space we call his "mind."

I conclude that the cognitive function of speech is to enable us to talk not only to others but to ourselves as well (and thus be our own interlocutor). Since this view runs counter to conventional wisdom, I offer a sobering analogy to support it.

Self-abuse and Self-conversation

For more than two hundred years—from the eighteenth century until the early part of the twentieth—sexual self-stimulation was regarded as an abnormal and dangerous practice and was called "self-abuse." Today, self-conversation is regarded as the symptom of an abnormal and dangerous mental state and is called "hearing voices" (or "auditory hallucination").[8]

Although these judgments rest on valid biological foundations, it is a mistake to treat these foundations as moral criteria for standards of social behavior. Until recent times, procreation depended on heterosexual, genital intercourse;* hence, it was reasonable to regard it as normal and to define any deviation from it—especially in the direction of what appeared to be self-sufficiency—as abnormal. The same goes for speech, whose biological-social function is to enable people to communicate without sight (that is, by words rather than gestures).

Of course, not everyone was fooled by the doctrine of masturbatory insanity. There were thoughtful and courageous persons who recognized that sexual self-satisfaction was not a horrible aberra-

---

*This is no longer the case. To be sure, artificial insemination is artificial only in the same sense in which contraception is artificial. Because everything we do occurs in nature and is, in that sense, natural, the distinction between the "natural" and the "artifical" is much more problematic than it may seem. By the same token, since all behavior has a function, there can be no "dysfunctional" behavior; the term is a scientistic euphemism for "disapproved."

tion but a harmless act. In 1879—in a short, satirical essay titled "The Science of Onanism"—Mark Twain mocked the conventional view of masturbation in lines such as the following:

Homer in the second book of the *Iliad* says with fine enthusiasm, "Give me masturbation or give me death!" . . . Robinson Crusoe says, "I cannot describe what I owe to this gentle art". . . . Cetewayo, the Zulu hero, remarked, "A jerk in the hand is worth two in the bush." The immortal Franklin has said, "Masturbation is the mother of invention."[9]*

And so Mark Twain went on, page after hilarious page. Sixty years later, Sigmund Freud went to his grave, still believing that masturbation caused mental illness.

The doctrine of masturbatory insanity is now virtually forgotten. Instead, the doctrine of hearing-voices-is-schizophrenia reigns supreme. Again, not everyone is fooled. There are thoughtful and courageous persons who recognize that self-conversation is not a psychiatric aberration but an ordinary act. After working on the Manhattan Project, Richard Feynman—one of the foremost physicists of our age—went to teach at Cornell University. A short time later he received an induction notice from his draft board. He loved to tell the story of his encounter with the psychiatrists who examined him for fitness for military service. James Gleick, Feynman's biographer, retells the story:

Stripped to his underwear, he goes from booth to booth, until—"Finally, we get to booth No. 13, Psychiatrist." Witch doctor. Baloney. Faker. Feynman held an extreme view of psychiatry. . . . [The psychiatrist begins by asking some pedantic questions.] Now a fourth question—*Do you think people talk about you?*—and Feynman detects that this is the routine: three innocent questions and then down to business.
"So I say, Yeah." The psychiatrist makes a note. . . . *Do you talk to yourself?* "I admitted that I do. . . . (Incidentally, I didn't tell him something which I can tell you, which is I find myself sometimes talking to myself in quite an elaborate fashion. . . .) 'The integral will be larger than this sum of the terms, so that would make the pressure higher, you see?' 'No, you're crazy.' 'No, I'm not! No, I'm not!' I say. I argue with myself. I have two voices that work back and forth." . . . *Do you hear voices in your head?* . . . "Very rarely." He admits a few occasions. Sometimes, in fact, just as he was

---

*This essay was not mentioned in Twain's early biographies. The piece was published only in 1976. To extol masturbation, sexologists now call it "self-pleasuring."

falling asleep, he would hear Edward Teller, with his distinctive Hungarian accent, in Chicago, giving him his first briefing on the atomic bomb.[10]

A second psychiatrist then examines Feynman. Same questions, same answers. This psychiatrist calls Feynman's hearing Teller's voice a "hypnagogic hallucination." Feynman is classified 4F.[11]

"Hearing Voices" as Self-deception

Feynman was an honest person, unwilling—indeed, unable—to lie to himself. In contrast, persons willing to deceive themselves are likely to interpret hearing voices in psychiatric terms, as "hearing voices." For example, Virginia Woolf, like Richard Feynman, also heard voices. There the similarities end.

Feynman was adventurous. Woolf was timid. In a letter to her close friend, Ethel Smyth, dated 22 June 1930, Woolf characterized herself thus: "I was always sexually cowardly. . . . My terror of real life has always kept me in the nunnery."[12] Her husband, Leonard, also acknowledged being a coward: "I was a coward and she [Virginia] was a snob."[13] The upshot was that Virginia and Leonard habitually deceived themselves and each other, especially about Virginia's "illness." It suited both to believe that, at certain times, Virginia (literally) "heard voices." In her fiction, and her fiction only, was she truthful about "madness."

I list herewith a few of Woolf's remarks pertinent to the matter of "voices": "I do not like the Jewish voice";[14] "How I hated marrying a Jew—how I hated their nasal voice."[15] Before writing *To the Lighthouse*, Woolf said that she "could hear her [mother's] voice, see her, imagine what she would do or say as I went about my day's doing." After finishing the novel, she stopped hearing her voice.[16]*

Note that Virginia Woolf identified what she considered to be Jewish voices as sounds, and hearing her mother's voice as a memory; in none of these instances did she interpret hearing voices as a manifestation of madness. However, when she wanted to identify herself as mad, she interpreted her experiences as "hearing voices," and vice versa. During her second "breakdown," following her father's death, she heard birds outside her window "singing in Greek."[17] In her last letter to her sister, Vanessa, she reported: "I

---

*Woolf's mother died when Virginia was thirteen and she never completely reconciled herself to that loss.

am certain now that I am going mad again. . . . I am always hearing voices."[18] And to Leonard she wrote: "I feel certain that I am going mad again. . . . I begin to hear voices, and I can't concentrate. . . . I can't read."[19]

Virginia Woolf understood only too well that creative writing requires solitude. Hence, she could have known that just as one cannot write a novel while listening to other voices at a party, so one cannot write (or read or concentrate) while listening to one's own inner voices. The question is: Why didn't she regard hearing the voices of her "madness" as imaginary, a manifestation of her preoccupation with her own thoughts, memories, and anxieties? I believe the answer is, because she did not want to. The examples I cited illustrate that Woolf chose to interpret hearing some voices as memory, and others as actual voices. She longed for her mother, loathed Jews, acknowledged harboring these sentiments, and re-membered the voices associated with them as imaginary. However, periodically she wanted to think of herself as mad, wanted others to think of her as mad, did not acknowledge harboring such wishes, chose to view her "madness" as psychiatrists view it, and dutifully referred to hearing voices in the language of psychiatry.[20]

There remains for me to mention one remark of Virginia Woolf's—the only one I found in her voluminous writings—that suggests that she understood that the voices the mad person hears are his own. In *The Writer's Diary*, she observed: "having reeled across the last ten pages [of *The Waves*] with some mo-ments of such intensity and intoxication that I seemed to stumble after my own voice, or almost after some sort of speaker (as when I was mad), I was almost afraid, remembering the voices that used to fly ahead."[21]

In short, Virginia Woolf feared not being able to control her "voices" (self-injurious thinking), much as some men fear not being able to control their violence (injurious actions).

CONTROLLING THOUGHT/SPEECH

For the young child, separation from the parent is a kind of death. Silence and solitude signify abandonment. It is imperative for the young child to not sever communicative connection with the adult on whom he depends. Hence, withholding information from the parent would be tantamount to a sort of semantic suicide. The child thus tells his parents everything, or believes that he does. That is why he believes that they know what is "in" his mind. As the child grows older, this conviction is usually replaced by the belief that God knows his mind, a belief that often persists throughout life.*

However, to establish his separate identity, the child must also move in the opposite direction, that is, he must learn to withhold certain types of information from parents, teachers, and other authorities. Only by having secrets—often a "private" diary—can the young person establish boundaries between himself and others. In short, he must learn how and when to keep his mouth shut. We forget that learning to not speak is a skill almost as important as learning to speak, and probably more difficult to achieve. According to the Russian linguist A. N. Sokolov, it is "an *art* which modern man acquires rather late in life."[22]

Still, our need for the Other is virtually unappeasable. Its ultimate manifestation is the longing for a union so intimate and secure that secrets between the self and the Other are unnecessary. The power of this fantasy of perfect love and understanding derives from the fear of facing the two ultimate realities of our existence, loneliness and death. Most people never acquiesce to these facts of life. Nor need they to. Religion teaches them that such acquiescence is a form of ignorance and wickedness. The godly person, who walks with Jesus, is never alone and never "dies."**

Religion and Self-conversation

Educated persons tend to underestimate the intensity of peoples' fears of finitude and solitude, and the ubiquity of their compensatory beliefs in the reality of "other lives" (especially life after death) and supernatural beings. According to a large 1994 Gallup Poll, 90 percent of Americans believe in heaven, 73 percent in hell, and 65 percent in the devil.[23] *Newsweek* reports that "Angels are appearing everywhere in America. . . . Those who see angels, talk to them, put others in touch with them are prized goods on television and radio talk shows."[24] Father Andrew Greeley, the sociologist-novelist, states that "Angels represent God's personal care for each one

---

*Modern totalitarian governments take advantage of this psychological vulnerability and elevate the individual's not having secrets from the state to a lofty principle of collectivist morality.

**The skeptical atheist—who accepts the futility of finding perfect security in God or man and welcomes the finality of death—is still a culturally aberrant person.

of us." The reporter perceptively adds: "The belief in angels implies that we are not alone in the universe." It also implies that we do not die. Says Lawrence S. Cunningham, chairman of the theology department at the University of Notre Dame: "When I die, I'll be very disappointed if I don't meet any angels." Sophy Burnham, the author of *A Book of Angels*—now in its thirtieth printing, with almost 600,000 copies sold—asserts: "We do not die! . . . This much I have seen with my own eyes."[25]

The results of a poll by *Time* magazine are consistent with these findings. Asked, "Which best describes what you believe angels to be?", 55 percent of the respondents answered: "Higher spiritual beings created by God with special powers to act as his agents on earth." Only 7 percent said: "Figments of the imagination." Thirty-two percent of the respondents stated that they have "personally felt an angelic presence," and 49 percent said they "believe in the existence of fallen angels, or devils." These true believers supported their views by explaining that "Those who have an angel story . . . couldn't make up the visions they saw."[26]

The Angel as Speaker

The English word "angel" comes from the Greek *angelos*, which means messenger. *Webster's* defines angel as a "supernatural messenger of God." In religious lore, angels are represented as singers in a heavenly choir and the bearers of good news. The devil, the "fallen angel," is a very different kind of messenger. His name, from the Greek *diabolos*, means slanderer. He is represented as a repulsive animal or as an adult male of vile appearance. His sole reason for being is to defy God. It will repay to briefly examine how he does his job.

Satan first appears in Genesis 3:1, as a serpent. He addresses Eve as follows: "Ye, hath God said, Ye shall not eat of every tree of the garden?"[27] Eve replies that there is but one tree in the Garden whose fruit God has forbidden. Satan perseveres: "And the serpent said unto the woman, Ye shall not surely die."[28] In other words, the devil taunts and tempts Eve to defy God by assuring her that God's warning is an empty threat, a scare-tactic.

The Gospel-writers explicitly equated sinning with being "of the devil."[29] However, if we view the colloquy between the serpent and Eve nontheologically, we could interpret the devil's communications as an invitation to leading a less restricted, more adventurous life. The Voice of the Devil is the voice that challenges, dares, taunts, and tempts: it invites man to yield to temptation and, implicitly, also to resist it by strengthening his control over himself. Eve and Adam yield. Job resists.

Nothing stops Satan. He tempts even God: "Then Satan answered the Lord, and said, Does Job fear God for nought?"[30] God accepts the challenge and makes Job the prototype of the man who welcomes suffering as his proof of loving God.

Satan tempts Jesus as well: "And when the tempter came to him, he said, If thou be the Son of God, command that these stones be made bread. But he answered and said, It is written, Man shall not live by bread alone, but by every word that proceedeth out of the mouth of God."[31]

There is a certain similarity between modern diet books, that train people to resist the temptation of gluttony, and the Bible, that teaches people to resist the temptations of liberty and lust. "Better to reign in hell," says Satan in Milton's *Paradise Lost*, "than serve in heaven."[32] The devil is the incarnation of evil because he is the Tempter, *par excellence*: He has "wiles," "devices," and "tricks"; he appeals to our ambition, curiosity, pride, and lust. We make a pact with him at our own peril.

The reciprocally opposing Voices of angels and the devil reflect the tension between the morality of childish obedience and adult self-responsibility.[33] For the ancients, temptation and the struggle for self-control was a moral problem with a religious solution. For us, it is a psychiatric problem with a pharmacological solution.[34]

God and Mind as Speakers

For many people, God, angels, and the devil are vivid realities; and so too are the mind and mental diseases. Although I regard supernatural beings and psychological abstractions as cognitive constructs, I respect the conviction of reality that attends them as testimony that they are based on something real: I believe that reality is the universal experience of talking to oneself. This elementary act lies at the heart of the ideas of both God and Mind:[35] Both ideas are anchored in the act of communication; both are manifestations of our inability to conceive of ourselves in terms other than as speakers-and-listeners.*

---

*Young children and the books written for them endow every animal and imaginary being with the power of speech.

A silent God—a God that never spoke, that never revealed His Will to man—would be a mockery of the very idea of God. Similarly, a mind that never spoke to the self—that did not think or remember—would not be a mind at all. "One may choose not to utter one's mind," observed Ambrose Bierce. "And if he do [sic] not sometimes choose to utter he will eventually cease to think. A mind without utterance is like a lake without an outlet; though fed with mountain springs and unfailing rivers, its waters do not long keep sweet."[36]

The view that God is the quintessential Speaker is supported by a careful rereading of Genesis. First, God creates darkness in a void. Things begin to happen only after He begins to speak: "And God said, Let there be light . . ." (1:3). The phrase, "And God said . . . ," is repeated nine times in chapter 1. To whom is God speaking, when there is no one to hear Him? Why is He speaking about what He will do, instead of just doing it? I believe that the linguistic format of Genesis,with its mantra-like repetition of the phrase, "And God said," reflects the Bible-writers' experience of talking to themselves, of inner speech preceding action, much as a promise preceded its fulfillment. Lastly, in Genesis God utters the First Lie: He promises to kill Adam and Eve if they eat of the Tree, but fails to do so. Perhaps He did not want to be left alone.

It must be noted that the God of the Old Testament speaks to Himself and does not disown His voice. Indeed, the idea of God "hearing voices" is at once obscene and incoherent: It is blasphemous to demean the Creator by making Him mad; and it is incoherent to attribute nonintentionality to Will incarnate.* As the great Russian linguist Mikhail Bakhtin emphasized, assuming responsibility for one's own Voice is one of the critical characteristics of human agency: "An independent, responsible, and active discourse is *the* fundamental indicator of an ethical, legal, and political human being."[37]

To be accepted as sane (normal), the individual must acknowledge his self-conversation as his own (thinking). Scientists may say that Nature or Science "tells" them such and such, but they do not disown these "tellings" and do not attribute them to external sources. Whereas prophets and (some) psychotic persons not only say that God is talking to them, they disown these "tellings" and attribute them to Voices outside themselves. If the speaker attrib-

---

*In the next chapter I shall show that it is similarly demeaning and incoherent to attribute nonresponsibility to the mind.

utes his voice to God, and if the Authorities-and-People believe that God indeed speaks to him, then they hail him as a Prophet; but if he makes the same attribution, and the Authorities-and-People believe that he is talking to himself, then they declare him to be mad and lock him up in an insane asylum. As I remarked some time ago: "If you talk to God, you are praying; if God talks to you, you have schizophrenia."[38]

In short, prayer is autologue *validated by religion*; whereas hallucination is autologue *invalidated by psychiatry*.

THE BIRTH OF THE INDIVIDUAL AND HIS MIND

Although neither "autologue" nor "self-conversation" is a part of the English vocabulary, we have a plethora of words that refer to the phenomenon of talking to oneself, such as believing, conjecturing, considering, contemplating, debating, deliberating, meditating, musing, pondering, presuming, reasoning, reflecting, ruminating, supposing, surmising, and, of course, thinking. Some of these terms—for example, pondering—apply only to self-conversation; others—for example debating—refer to speech acts that may be carried out either alone or with others.

Recognizing the ubiquity of self-conversation is an indispensable antidote against the currently conventional view that regards (normal) speech as a verbal act that one person directs to another person or persons (as formerly conventional view regarded [normal] sexual activity as a genital act that one person engages in with another person (of the opposite sex); and that classifies some inner dialogues as normal (meditating, reflecting), and others as abnormal (hearing voices, being plagued by invasive thoughts).

Appraising Our Self-conversations

Like any experience, the experience of listening to another person or to oneself may be satisfying or unsatisfying. If it is pleasant, the experience presents no problems and need not be considered here. However, if it is unpleasant, it presents a very serious problem indeed.

If listening to the Other is disagreeable—because his discourse is boring, irritating, or otherwise irksome—we can protect ourselves in various ways, depending on our relationship to the speaker; for example, we can leave, ask or order him to keep quiet, tune him out, or fall asleep. If the offended person possesses legal power to coerce the offending Other (and is willing to use it), he may silence him by force, for example by incarcerating or executing him. The voices of heretics were often quelled by first tearing out their tongues and then killing them.

If listening to ourselves is disagreeable—because our inner voice pesters us with annoying orders or accuses us of wickedness—we cannot readily escape from the speaker, nor can we still his voice by banishing him. How do we cope with this problem? How does society appraise the various methods we use to silence the troublesome inner speaker?

Before answering these questions, I want to note that, luckily, much of the time we are satisfied with our inner dialogue, a situation reflected by the terms we use to describe it, such as pondering, planning, reflecting, remembering. There are many times, however, when we are dissatisfied with it. For example, when we must wait for the results of an important medical test, we may feel compelled to ruminate about certain difficult choices we might have to make and thus neglect our other interests. One way to cope with such a predicament is by applying our attention to an absorbing task, such as working or meeting pressing family obligations. Another way is to sedate ourselves with a psychoactive drug, such as alcohol, opium, Valium, Haldol, and so forth. If we are unable to silence our troubling inner speech or deafen our troubled inner hearing in these ways, then we find ourselves confronted, so to speak, with an interlocutor from whose tormenting there is no escape. A person so (self-) tortured is likely to exhibit behaviors similar to those displayed by Lady Macbeth—and solve his problem by killing himself. Or he may attribute his troubling thoughts to others (individuals or illnesses)—and solve his problem by persecuting his personal or medical "enemies."

In short, the use of psychoactive drugs is man's oldest and culturally most widely shared method for *altering* his inner dialogue, and suicide is his ultimate method for *terminating* it.

Perhaps because these matters deeply disturb the normal person's peace of mind, psychiatrists and psychologists have invented, and the public has embraced, a pseudomedical jargon to describe certain unwanted self-conversations as the manifestations of "diseased minds." As a result, it is virtually impossible to give a faithful account of these phenomena. Professionals and lay persons alike thus believe certain fundamentally false "facts," such as that hallucinating persons "hear voices" or that obsessional persons have ideas that "invade" their "consciousness."[39] For example, Rosenhan and Seligman's widely used *Abnormal Psychology* states: "Obsessions are repetitive thoughts, images, or impulses that *invade consciousness*, are often abhorrent, and are very difficult to dismiss or control."[40] However, terms such as "thoughts," "images," and "impulses" do not name entities (like microbes), endowed with energy enabling them to invade another entity (the mind); nor does the term "consciousness" name an entity or territory that could be invaded by an enemy. The microbial metaphor falsifies the facts. The terms "thoughts," "images," and "impulses" refer to self-conversations. We call certain thoughts "obsessive" because the person is "obsessed" with them, that is, they dominate his attention (and, of course, he cannot control or suppress them). However, everyone interested in a particular subject is more or less preoccupied by thinking about it. Sport buffs think about athletics, music lovers about symphonies, doctors about diseases and patients, and so on.

My point is not that there is no difference between normal interest and abnormal rumination, but that both are self-conversations. It is a mistake to regard some self-reflections (such as an individual's interest in his work or hobby) as inner dialogues, and others (such as his obsession about cleanliness) as mental diseases. So-called hallucinations, hypochondriacal preoccupations, obsessional thoughts, and so forth are all instances of self-conversations.

It is also an error to frame these phenomena in terms of the subject's alleged inability to control his thoughts. Talking to oneself, like talking to another person, is an activity. Thinking (talking)—like drawing a picture or throwing a ball—is a voluntary act. This does not mean that deciding to have one thought rather than another is like deciding whether to wear one tie or another. Most of our thinking, like most of our behavior, is routine and automatic; and much of our nonroutine behavior is also spontaneous and, in that sense, unwilled. When an artist or scientist has a seemingly unintended (good) idea, we say he is "inspired" and call him a "genius"; but when an ordinary person has an unintended (bad) thought, we say he "hears voices" and call him "mentally ill" (and attribute "it" to brain disease). This cannot be so. It is absurd to imagine that the brain can distinguish between two acts that are similar in all important respects except our moral judgments of them—for example, between lighting a match to set fire in one's fireplace and lighting a match to set one's house on fire.

Mind in the Mirror of Language

Equipped with an idea of soul, medieval philosophy had no need for the mind, which came into its own only with the birth of the modern notions of the individual or self. *The Oxford English Dictionary (OED)* defines "mind" (the noun) as "The seat of a person's consciousness. . . . The soul as distinguished from the body," and cites John Locke's use of it in 1690 as an early example: "Due care being had to keep the Body in Strength and Vigour, so that it may be able to obey and execute the Orders of the Mind." It is this use, not Descartes', that illustrates the dichotomy between body and mind. It is important to note that, *qua* entity, the mind, like the soul, is immediately equated with God. The *OED* cites Locke writing in 1690: "That eternal infinite Mind, who made and governs all Things"; and Pope writing in 1732: "The great directing Mind of All ordains."[41]

The idea of the person as individual, rather than as a member of a family or clan, is a relatively late Western development. When the Founders wrote the Constitution, the word "autobiography" was not yet a part of the English language.* The *OED* gives 1809 as the earliest date for the appearance of the modern use of this word, that is, denoting a narrative construction of the self, rather than a narrative of the soul's relation with God.[42] "Taking a world view," concludes anthropologist Colin Morris, "one might almost regard it [individualism] as an eccentricity among cultures."[43]

The word "self" is only a little older. According to the *OED*, the term "first appears as a living formative element about the middle of the sixteenth century. The number of *self*-compounds was greatly augmented toward the middle of the seventeenth century . . . since the prefix is of unlimited application, no attempt has been made to represent with fullness the extent to which it has been employed." The *OED* lists fifty-two half-columns of words with the prefix *self*, but self-conversation is not among them.

As I noted in the Preface, prior to the sixteenth century, the English word "mind" functioned only as a verb. There was then no English word for mind as noun, just as there is still no German or French word for it. In modern English, countless words—for example, bug, drug, hug, mug—function as both verb and noun;

---

*The *OED* lists the word "autology" as the term used in the seventeenth century to denote self-knowledge.

the verb refers to what the person does (action), the noun, to an event or object (outside the self). Because nouns such as "bug" or "hug" name real objects or events, we *understand* that "bugging" a person means annoying him, and that hugging him means giving him a hug; and because the noun "mind" names a fictitious object, we *misunderstand* "minding" as using our "mind."* But we *have* no minds. Instead, we, *qua* living persons, *mind*. How and what we mind is who we are. Minding is quintessentially our own business. The greatest indignity a person can inflict on another is to treat him as if he could not mind, that is, as if he had no mind "of his own" and hence his mind/minding was no longer his business. Similarly, the greatest injury a person can inflict on himself is to treat his mind as if its business were not worth minding, that is, as if it were no longer his, and hence perceive his own actions as the results of the mindings of others.

Because people whose language is German and French have no word for mind as a noun, they are better protected from reifying "mind" as an entity or identifying "it" with the brain. The German term *Verstand* is often translated as mind. However, *Verstand* literally means understanding and is so devoid of the connotations of the English word "mind" that it would be incoherent to say that *Verstand* is the brain. The cognate German words *Geist* and *Seele* mean spirit and soul, not mind; only when combined with *Krankheit* (illness)—as in *Geisteskrankheit* and *Seelenkrankheit*—do these terms mean "mental" (illness).

The fact that there is no French noun corresponding to the English "mind" is perhaps even more remarkable, inasmuch as the adjective *mentale* is used exactly as we use the term "mental": mental illness is *maladie mentale*. When the French need a mind-like noun, they use *esprit* (spirit), *pensée* (thought), *âme* (soul), *mentalité* (quality of mind), and *idée* (idea), or employ phrases such as *état d'esprit* (mental state) or *manière de penser* (turn of mind). Revealingly, the Latin root *mens* also serves as the basis of the French words for lying as in *mensonge* (lie) and *mentir* (to lie).

---

*If the noun "mind" is used to mean brain, then of course it does name an object. In that terminology, brains "mind," and persons—other than the scientist who uses such language—cease to exist.

Pioneer Philosophers of the Mind

Imbued with classical learning as well as Augustinian philosophy, Petrarch (Francesco Petrarca, 1304–1374)—the Renaissance poet-philosopher who is often called "the first humanist"—was perhaps the first modern to recognize the inherent connections between mind and language and oppose the literal interpretation of the medical metaphor of rhetorical healing.

Christianity borrowed the idea of the healing word from the classic world and made it its own. In 1 Thessalonians 4:18, for example, the faithful are exhorted: "Wherefore, comfort one another with these words." "The rhetorical realm of consoling, fairly strong in certain Fathers," writes George W. McClure, "gave way to the offices of communion, confession and penance, extreme unction."[44]

Petrarch perfected the office of rhetorical consoler on the basis, revealingly, of his reflections and experiences as a self-consoler. McClure explains that, for Petrarch, "the written, spoken, and contemplative word is the true medicine for self-healing," and cites the following passage: "I cannot tell you what worth are to me in solitude certain familiar and famous words not only grasped in the mind but *actually spoken orally*, words with which I am accustomed to rouse my sleepy thoughts."[45]

Petrarch maintained that "The care of the mind calls for the philosopher" and that doctors—whose job is to use "herbs not words"—should confine themselves to the cure of bodies and "leave the cure or moving of minds to the true philosophers and orators."[46]

Michel de Montaigne (1533–1592) appears to be the first European to celebrate self-conversation as true inner peace or, as he put it, "liberty." "We have," he wrote, "a soul capable of turning in on itself; it can keep itself company."[47] His advice to older people was: "We should set aside an *arrièreboutique*, a room, just for ourselves, at the back of the shop, keeping it entirely free and founding there our true liberty."[48]

The thought of Giambattista Vico (1668–1744)—a professor of rhetoric at the University of Naples—is important for our consideration because he introduced into modern philosophy the viewpoint that "a systematic science of mind [is] identical with the history of its development and growth," and that "This could be traced only through investigation of the changing symbols—words, monuments, works of art, laws and customs, and the like—in which mind expressed itself."[49] By identifying mind as the sum total of what a person does and says, Vico transcended, once and for all, the so-called Cartesian mind-body dualism.

The Platonic idea that the mind is thinking was rediscovered and made explicit by Immanuel Kant (1728–1804). In 1798, he wrote: "Every man . . . thinks of the cadaver, which is no longer himself, as himself in the shadowy grave or somewhere else. This illusion cannot be dispelled: *it lies in the nature of thinking as a talking to and about oneself. . . . To think is to talk to oneself.*"[50]*

Familiarity with German facilitates this recognition, since that language possesses a term, *Selbstgespräch*, that means precisely talking to oneself. Probably because there is no analogous word in English—and because we do not recognize the phenomenon as an ordinary activity—*Cassell's* German-English dictionary mistranslates *Selbstgespräch* as "monologue, soliloquy," activities that *Selbstgespräch* is emphatically not.

The German-British philologist, Friedrich Max Müller (1823–1900)—famous in his time—picked up Kant's theme and made it his own. He wrote: "Some of the Polynesians would seem to have a far truer insight into the nature of thought and language than some of our modern philosophers, for they call thinking 'speaking in the stomach.'"[51] Anticipating Gilbert Ryle by a century, Müller offered the following rebuttal to those who would locate the mind in the brain:

We cannot see without the eye, or hear without the ear; . . . but neither can the eye see, or the ear hear . . . without the will of what we call our self. To look for the faculty of speech in the brain would, in fact, be hardly less Homeric than to look for the soul in the midriff. . . . The brain may be a sine qua non of intellect, as the eye is of sight, and the ear is of sound, but as little as the eye can see and the ear can hear, can the brain think.[52]

Among contemporary scholars, the person who best articulated the significance of the dialogic character of speech is Mikhail Bakhtin. He wrote:

The fact is that when the listener perceives and understands the meaning of speech, he simultaneously takes an active, responsive attitude toward it. He either agrees or disagrees with it (completely or partially), augments

*The original reads: "denn sie liegt in der Natur des Denkens, als eines Sprechens zu und von sich selbst. . . . Denken ist reden mit sich selbst."

it, applies it, prepares for its execution, and so on. . . . Any understanding of live speech . . . necessarily elicits it [a response], in one form or another: the listener becomes the speaker.[53]

Bakhtin's insight that "The listener becomes the speaker" explains both our ability and inability to understand the Other. We understand him, if we want to assume a responsive attitude toward his voice, because we love, like, or respect him, or want him to love, like, or respect us. People who are fond of each other often say, "We *understand* each other."

Conversely, we do not understand the Other, if we reject assuming a responsive attitude toward his voice, because we regard him as insane or otherwise unworthy of being listened to. As the sympathetic listener becomes the comprehending hearer, so the unsympathetic listener becomes the uncomprehending hearer; He distances and disidentifies himself from the speaker and experiences difficulty understanding him. This phenomenon is writ large in the relationship between the psychiatrist and his psychotic patient.* Although psychiatrists are reputed to be especially understanding and adept at decoding the communications of mentally disordered persons, actually the opposite is more often the case. It is the social mandate of the mental health professional to define the (crazy) Other's speech as gibberish, the unintelligible discharge of his diseased brain.

In a famous experiment, conducted by Stanford psychology professor David Rosenhan, a group of normal volunteers, pretending to be crazy, got themselves admitted to a mental hospital. Once defined as mental patients, the hospital staff interpreted the volunteers' ordinary behavior as symptoms of insanity. Rosenhan concluded: "It is clear that we cannot distinguish the sane from the insane *in* psychiatric hospitals."[54]

In a dialogue, speaker and listener form a reciprocating dyad or pair. "What is heard and actively understood," wrote Bakhtin, "will find its response in the subsequent speech or behavior of the listener."[55] Sokolov put it thus: "The hearing of speech is not simply hearing. To a certain degree we, as it were, speak together with the speaker."[56] This process is at work with respect to the printed word as well.

---

*The relationship between the bureaucrat and his suplicant, especially if the latter is a foreigner or a member of a despised minority, is another example.

Echoing Müller's credo that "Language and the word are almost everything in human life,"[57] Bakhtin added: "For the word (and, consequently, for a human being) there is nothing more terrible than a *lack of response*."[58] Lack of response severs the linguistic bond between the reciprocating pair intrinsic to dialogue. Our deep-seated dread of silence-as-loneliness explains why religion and madness—faith-and-prayer and hearing-and-talking-to-Voices—are two of the most enduring elements in human life. They constitute the "cures," as it were, for the elemental human fear of death as existential-semantic abandonment.

2

Responsibility: Self-blame and Self-praise

Since the Enlightenment and the birth of modern science, educated people have been expected to embrace the rationalist doctrine of determinism and deny the reality of free will and individual responsibility. Yet, reflection tells us that there is little difference between the certainty with which we know that we are alive and the certainty with which we know that we are responsible.

RESPONSIBILITY: THE PARADIGMATIC SELF-CONVERSATION

Science commences when people begin to pay attention to certain regularities in their environment. The most elementary regularities in nature are sunrise and sunset, which is why astronomy—the study of the planets—is the oldest science. The most elementary regularities in human nature are our experiences of willing and being responsible, which is why religion—the regulation of intentionality and culpability—is the oldest social institution.

For millennia, man lived in a technologically undeveloped world over which he had scant control. His experience of pervasive helplessness contradicted his intense sense of willing, which he projected unto imaginary spirits. He thus saw natural events through intention-colored lenses and attributed them to quasi-human agents (gods). In such a view of the world, nothing happens "naturally"; instead, everything is willed, by human or, more often, supra-human, agents. Animism—attributing, say, death due to disease to the will of a hostile person or spirit—thus magnifies, indeed universalizes, intentionality and culpability.

In contrast, modern man lives in a technologically sophisticated world over which he—and others, possessing specialized knowledge and technics—has far-reaching control. Yet, his experience of technological control over nature is contradicted by his intense sense of personal helplessness in an increasingly crowded and complex world. The scientifically enlightened person thus denies free will and personal responsibility and replaces them with the notion of "psychological determinism" (as Freud called it). In such a view of the world, nothing (or almost nothing) happens as a result of human choice; instead, everything is due to causes, most of which remain to be identified by a better understanding of the neurobiology of the brain. Scientism—attributing, say, suicide to genes or neurotransmitters—thus reduces or annuls intentionality and culpability.[1]

Happily, there is a middle ground between animism and scientism. We can distinguish events that require a causal account or scientific explanation, such as the fall of an apple, from acts that require a motivational account and moral judgment, such as the Fall of Man. Making this distinction, as Michael Oakeshott emphasized, is a prerequisite for the proper study of human conduct: "[T]he movement of a human eyelid is a categorically ambiguous identity; it may be a wink or it may be a blink, a wink which is an exhibition of intelligence, a subscription to a 'practice' and has a reason, and a blink which is a component of a 'process' to be understood in terms of a 'law' or a 'cause.'"[2] Because human interest colors our perception of reality, virtually any human act may appear to be—or may be made to seem to be—"categorically ambiguous." Thus, for the conspiracy theorist, all blinks that excite his interest are winks: he attributes responsibility for events that upset him to agents not responsible for them. Conversely, for the modern neuroscientist, as I shall show, blinks and winks are both blinks: he attributes responsibility for human action to brains and minds, not persons.[3]

The problem we perpetually face is, When should we attribute "mentality" to a person, treat his behavior as an intentional act, and hold him responsible for it? And when should we attribute "materiality" to him, treat his behavior as a manifestation of physical processes in his body, and hold him not responsible for it? The same questions may be posed about our attitude toward ourselves: When should we treat ourselves as responsible agents, and when as nonresponsible victims (of mental illness or some other cause)? It is an illusion that we can avoid this choice, that when we come to this fork in the road, we can—as Yogi Berra counseled—take it.

The point of these reflections is that while the physicist's choice between complementary explanations of natural phenomena is morally unproblematic,* the moral philosopher's choice between complementary explanations of personal behavior is ethically oner-ous. Since everyone is his own moral philosopher, everyone finds this choice onerous and, not surprisingly, many people are eager to evade it.

Responsibility: Answering the Other and the Self

We use the word "responsible" to refer to three quite different things: a (physical) cause, (moral) blameworthiness, and (legal) culpability. For example, we say that lightning was responsible for setting a forest on fire (cause); that Jones was responsible for (unintentionally) burning down his house, because he fell asleep while smoking (blunder, fault); and that Smith was responsible for (intentionally) burning down his house, because he wanted to collect the insurance on it (crime). I shall be concerned with the moral and legal uses of the term only. Although individual respon-sibility is an attribute of persons, we often use the term "mind" in lieu of the word "person," and attribute responsibility or its absence to "it."

The word "responsible" comes from the Latin *respondere*, which means to respond or answer (hence its synonym, "answerable"). Although we often say that a person "has" responsibility, that locution is misleading: responsibility is not something that a person "has"; it is something that he "is" or is "said to be." Responsibility—like, say, loyalty—is a moral and psychological trait with which a *person* may or may not be accredited. Thus, a physician can examine a person's body to determine whether his kidney function is diminished or absent, because of renal disease; but he cannot examine a person's mind to determine whether "its" responsibility

---

*I refer here to Bohr's principle of complementarity, for example, the choice between interpreting light as composed of particles or of waves.

is diminished or annulled, because of mental disease (although that is precisely what the mental health professional pretends to do).

In religion, ethics, and law a person is regarded as a moral agent only if he is answerable for his conduct, here and in the hereafter, to God, Pope, King, the law, and his fellow man. Being responsible is thus a type of minding, like thinking and remembering. It follows that we must not credit "mindless" persons—that is, individuals unable to mind—with moral agency, lest they perish or be punished unjustly. Instead, we must treat them paternalistically.[4]* There is, indeed, a long tradition in English law, with roots in Roman law, of regarding infants, idiots, and the insane as mindless (mentally incompetent) and therefore lacking moral agency. To this list, contemporary American custom and law have added not only (many) so-called mental patients but also many "normal" persons—typically, the "victims" of their own bad habits—as (more or less or temporarily) mindless and hence lacking moral agency. I shall return to this subject presently. For now, let us keep our eye on the fact that we treat adults (unless they have been declared mentally incompetent by a court of law) as responsible for their behavior—and that we regard this arrangement as indispensable for social order in a just society.

This is precisely the conclusion at which Michael Polanyi** arrives in his *magnum opus, Personal Knowledge.* "So far as we know," he wrote, "the tiny fragments of the universe embodied in man are the only centers of thought and responsibility in the visible world. If that be so, the appearance of the human mind has been so far the ultimate stage in the awakening of the world."[5] It is also precisely the message that Pope John Paul II delivered in his 1955 encyclical letter "Evangelium Vitae." He stated: "Each individual in fact has moral responsibility for the acts which he personally performs; no one can be exempted from this responsibility, and on the basis of it everyone will be judged by God himself."[6]***

Note that Polanyi brackets responsibility with mind, and that the Pope brackets it with God.[7]

Webster's defines paternalism as a relationship "involving care and control suggestive of those followed by a father."

**Polanyi was trained as a physician in Hungary, became a world famous physical chemist in Berlin, and had a distinguished second career as a social philosopher in Manchester, England.

***As I shall presently show, the Church fails to adhere to this precept, automatically exempting from responsibility for his deed anyone who kills himself.

Conscience: The Lawmaker and Judge Within

The answerability of the person as moral agent is not limited to interrogation by external authorities. The sternest and most inescapable judge of a person's behavior is often his own self, monitoring not only his publicly observable actions, but his thoughts (self-conversations) as well. We call this personal judge the conscience. Minus the prefix *con*, we have *science*. Conscience, then, is that part of the mind that "knows." In contrast to the knowledge we call "information" or "memory," we call the knowledge of the conscience "moral judgment" or "knowing the difference between right and wrong." Moreover, the conscience does not merely comprehend, it also controls: it is the Voice that prompts us to do right and persecutes us for doing wrong.*

We call the "gnawing distress arising from a sense of guilt for past wrongs" (*Webster's*) "remorse," which comes from the Latin *re-mordere*, meaning to bite again. The German word for remorse is *Gewissensbisse* (*Gewissen* is conscience, *beissen* is to bite). This oral-aggressive image of biting seems deeply embedded in our notion of a tormenting conscience. Remorse, then, is the inner voice denouncing the self as an unjust-wicked agent. Similarly, as I shall discuss in the next chapter, revenge is the inner voice denouncing the Other as an unjust-wicked agent.

In this connection, it is important to note that Bishop Joseph Butler (1692–1752)—perhaps the most important premodern moral philosopher—extolled conscience as the emblem of moral agency, the characteristic that distinguishes human beings from animals. He identified conscience as a "superior principle of reflection"

which passes judgment upon himself and them; pronounces determinately some actions to be in themselves just, right, good; others to be in themselves evil, wrong, unjust: which, without being consulted, without being advised with, magisterially exerts itself, and approves or condemns him the doer accordingly. . . . It is by this faculty, natural to man, that he is a moral agent, that he is a law to himself.[8]

Butler then proposed a distinction between man and animals that is still the best we have. He wrote:

*I am couching this description in metaphoric language. The reifications and personifications implied are verbal devices, not the names of actual somatic entities.

It does not appear, that brutes have the least reflex sense of actions, as distinguished from events: or that will and design, which constitute the very nature of actions as such, are at all an object to their perception. But to ours they are: and they are the object, and the only one, of the approving and disapproving faculty. Acting, conduct, behaviour . . . is itself the natural object of the moral discernment . . . Intention of such and such consequences, indeed, is always included; for it is part of the action itself. . . . Animals, unlike men, do not appear capable of reflecting on their actions. Note the important distinction between event and action. An action implies "will" and "design."[9]

In short, conscience is a particular kind of self-conversation, the self's inner dialogue concerning the goodness or badness of its own conduct. How does our conscience—that is, how do we—know how to do this? The same way we know everything else, namely, by learning.

Learning to be Responsible

Newborn infants are human beings but, because they lack knowledge of right or wrong, are not moral agents. Soon after birth, however, parents begin to attribute a measure of responsibility to the child, for example, to tolerate progressively less frequent feedings or to sleep through the night. They do so not because the child is responsible for his behavior, but because they want him to become responsible for it, that is, they want him to acquire certain habits. The fact that human beings as well as animals can be trained rests precisely on the fact that responsibility is, *inter alia*, a trait an actor is expected to possess, rather than one that he possesses. Indeed, the habit-forming power of the *expectation of responsibility* is one of its most important features.

There is nothing novel in this observation. With his eyes on children, philosopher Arnold S. Kaufman observed: "One may be justified in blaming or praising an infant in order to influence his future behavior, but there would be no justice in it."[10] With his eyes on adults, economist Friedrich von Hayek asserted: "[T]he statement that a person is responsible for what he does aims at making his actions different from what they would be if he did not believe it to be true. We assign responsibility to a man, not in order to say that as he was he might have acted differently, but in order to make him different."[11] Finally, with his eyes on God, C. S. Lewis remarked: "Christ died for men precisely because men are *not* worth dying for; to make them worth it."[12]

The child's acquisition of a sense of responsibility runs roughly parallel to his acquisition of other types of knowledge and skills. In the course of this process, called "socialization," he is subjected to a succession of authorities who tell him what he may and may not do. Soon, he internalizes their voices and begins to tell himself what he may and may not do. This "inner voice" is, *par excellence*, the voice of the conscience; it is also the voice, so to speak, of everything we know or think. Unless the voices the child hears are unreasonably inhibiting, his self-conversations encompass everything that interests him. If the young person is exposed to inspiring voices and is himself inspired, the result of his autologues is likely to be great art or great science. In his old age, Isaac Newton (1642–1727) offered this explanation for his discoveries: "All this was in the two plague years of 1665 and 1666, for in those days I was in the prime of my age for invention, and *minded* mathematics and philosophy more than at any time since."[13]

To become educable, the child must be taught to be obedient. His obedience is considered to be a virtue. The phrase, "I was only following orders"—which became infamous during the postwar period—originates in this universal childhood experience. Freed from its association with Nazism, the claim is morally neutral and may be invoked either as a justification for right-doing (ordered by a virtuous conscience) or as an excuse for wrongdoing (ordered by a wicked superior). Conscientious objectors, whose moral principles tell them that war is evil, are excused from military service; non-conscientious objectors, whose pleasure-principle tells them that war is vexatious, are not. Martin Luther and Adolf Eichmann were both "following orders."[14]

Although every child is taught to be (more or less) obedient, he is usually *also* taught to be disobedient, to resist the blandishments of strangers, avoid imitating the fashionable (mis)behaviors of his peers, and distrust the ill-informed instructions of his teachers. Such disobedience is considered to be a virtue. Young people, in short, are enjoined both to think and not think for themselves. Voltaire satirized this dilemma with the following colloquy:

BOLDEMIND: All you have to do is learn to think. . . . Every man can educate himself. . . . Dare to think for yourself.

MEDROSO: They say that if everybody thought for himself it would result in a strange confusion.[15]

The paradox may be partly transcended by keeping in mind that, for the child, autonomy is not a valid option. It is a prerogative of the adult only.* Children and adults inhabit the same world in a physical sense only. Existentially, they live in different worlds. The child's universe is his family, whose members nurture, teach, reward, and punish him. Living outside the realm of adult responsibility, the child is, for the most part, not accountable to the laws of the larger society. This arrangement reflects the universal recognition that before children can engage in the life of society, they must be taught to understand and helped to conform their conduct to its rules. We intuitively grasp that a disobedient child is likely to be "unreasonably" defiant, that is, disobedient only for the sake of asserting his own will; we call him "willful." Whereas a (civilly) disobedient adult, capable of evaluating his options, is likely to have decided, for his own reasons, to disobey the Other's orders and suffer the consequences for good or ill; we call him "conscientious."

The theater that is society houses two separate auditoriums, one for children, another for adults. In each, different actors perform in different plays, before different audiences. In the children's drama—scripted by adults—obedience to the playwright's authority is a virtue and, if need be, an excuse as well. In the adults' drama—scripted by the performers—different audiences are likely to have different opinions about what constitutes virtue and vice. The distinctions we make between various degrees of responsibility, attributing less to some persons and more to others, rests on this fundamental division of life into childhood and adulthood.** The result is not a set of "facts" about individuals, but a set of moral judgments that society renders about them.

TEMPTATION AND SELF-CONTROL

To overcome his dependence on authority and become an independent adult, the child must learn to control himself, a task that requires overcoming two different kinds of obstacles, one posed by objects, the other by persons. The physical obstacles to self-control

*I recognize that the transition between childhood and adulthood is gradual; that autonomy is not an all-or-nothing quality; and that independence is the prize for making it in life, and dependence the consolation prize for not making it.

**Entrepreneurs advertise and sell to (competent) adults, but "prey" on (incompetent) children and old people.

are intrinsic to the human body and the natural world—that is, the neuromuscular immaturity of the child, the physical limitations of the adult body, and the dangers to life and limb posed by cold, fire, water, and other hazards. The human barriers to self-control are intrinsic to human nature and society—that is, the psychosocial immaturity of the child, the physiologically and socially generated drives and aspirations of the adult, and the dangers to life, liberty, and property posed by other people and social conventions. The child acquires self-control by learning to regulate the movements of his body, in particular, his limbs, his bladder, his bowel, and his organs of speech; by learning to avoid physical dangers, such as fire; and by learning to resist temptations, such as yielding indiscriminately to his aggressive, alimentary, or sexual urges.

Regardless of how successfully a person masters these obstacles, his dependence on others never ceases. Man cannot live by bread alone. He needs the Other and perishes without him. Our need for the Other, moreover, is closely connected with our being susceptible to him as a tempter. Hence, we must master the task of coping with temptations, striking a balance between yielding and resisting them, and retaining a measure of self-control consistent with our need for autonomy.

Although the theme of temptation lies at the heart of the biblical story of the origin of man as *person* or *responsible agent*; and although there is a plethora of adages and aphorisms about it—the subject of temptation is surprisingly neglected in the literature of psychology and psychiatry.

Coping with Temptation

The infant communicates by crying, which is a biologically preformed mechanism for attracting the parent's attention and assistance. Long before a baby learns to speak, he learns to wail, seemingly at will. His wailing is the paradigm of pro-vocation. The fact that parents are so easily provoked by the wailing of their own infants—and even by the wailing of infants not their own—makes good biological sense. Wailing is the infant's sole protection against both internal and external dangers, a weapon of self-defense whose use the parent may soon experience as an aggression against him.[16] That is why parents and parent-surrogates with poor self-control who are desperate to stop a child from crying sometimes injure and kill him in the process.

The preverbal child is a powerful provoker, but is relatively immune to provocation, except by strong noise or direct bodily stimulation. Only after he acquires speech does the child become provokable by words, and hence temptable—which we call "educable" or "teachable," if we approve his yielding, and call "corruptible" or "seduceable," if we do not.

We know that children are more teachable than adults. Why is this so? Neurophysiological reasons aside, their incentives for learning—to please themselves by pleasing a parent and to satisfy their curiosity—are more intense than those of adults. For the same reasons, they are also more temptable, which is why teaching them self-control is so important. It is also why, because no one completely outgrows the child in him, many maxims mock our helplessness vis-à-vis temptation. The Christian prays not to be led into temptation (Matthew 6:13), and acknowledges that "blessed is the man that endureth temptation" (James 1:12). The cynic, epitomized by Oscar Wilde, quips: "I can resist everything except temptation."* The connoisseur of wit savors Mark Twain's genius: "There are several good protections against temptation, but the surest is cowardice."

An individual's ability to cope with temptation is a good test of his self-control. Most human encounters contain an element of tempting-and-being-tempted or can be viewed in such terms. For example, the advertiser and merchant provoke a desire for goods or services; the coach and teacher, for mastery and knowledge; the pornographer, for sex; and so forth. The provoked person must choose whether to resist or yield to the temptation. This description presupposes that tempter and tempted alike are free and responsible agents—the former to tempt or not, the latter to resist or yield. But do tempter and tempted stand on morally equal footing? Or, as Shakespeare put it: "The tempter or the tempted, who sins most?"17

As a rule, it is easier to resist tempting than temptation. This renders the balance of power between the two parties experientially unequal. From this experiential inequality we infer that they must be morally unequal as well, the tempter being more blameworthy and culpable for his choosing to seduce than the tempted for his choosing to succumb to the enticement. As a result, we tend to disjoin rights and responsibilities, exemplified by punishing the

*He also said: "The only way to get rid of temptation is to yield to it."

sellers of certain goods and services, but not the buyers.[18] "We're just saying"—explained a Colombian judge, apropos of the decriminalization of the use of cocaine in that country in 1994—"that the person who consumes drugs is a victim and that the person who traffics in drugs is still a criminal."[19]

To this judge, and to the American public whom he was addressing, it is self-evident that the drug seller is a powerful adult (a "trafficker"), who is responsible for his behavior; and that the drug buyer is a powerless child-like person (a "patient"), who is not (fully or at all) responsible for his behavior. Indeed, it is now conventional wisdom to treat the producers and providers of many goods and services as responsible for the harms that people might suffer as a result of purchasing the goods and services the sellers offer. Examples abound. We treat individuals who manufacture cigarettes and operate casinos as businessmen responsible for their behavior, but treat individuals who smoke cigarettes and gamble (and lose) as child-like patients not responsible for their behavior. Lawmakers, judges, juries, the media, and the public consider this policy not merely morally desirable but "scientific." It is neither. It is simply a decision to treat one set of adults as morally competent persons who ought to be punished for offering a truthfully labeled product or service for sale in the market, and to treat another set of adults as morally incompetent persons who ought to be excused for yielding to certain ("irresistible") temptations;* and to use this distinction to punish and discourage certain behaviors, and reward and encourage certain other behaviors. With the naivest of conceits, we regard this disjunctive attribution of responsibility as both natural and just. Actually, it is a pathetic rationalization of our confusion about how best to cope with the complex risks inherent in modern life.

[margin annotation: Writers should quit using "we" this way. It is a contradiction because it excludes themselves and their supporters.]

The Parable of the Fall

To place the problem of risk-managing temptation in perspective, let us briefly reconsider our culture's paradigmatic scenario of it,

*This perspective concerning certain classes of voluntary exchanges represents an inversion of the classic moral principle of *caveat emptor* (buyer beware) and exemplifies today's conventional wisdom's animosity against personal responsibility. Until recently, the policy of punishing the seller and excusing the buyer was confined to the illegal trade in sex (prostitution).

the parable of the Fall. The drama begins when Satan challenges Eve to eat the Forbidden Fruit. Eve hesitates, fearing God's punishment: "God hath said, Ye shall not eat of it, neither shall ye touch it, lest ye die" (Genesis 3:3). Satan reassures her that God will welsh on his threat: "And the serpent said unto the woman, Ye shall not surely die" (3:4). The rest, as they say, is history. We could interpret this grand parable in several ways, for example as the first historical case of the following:

- *Child abuse:* Lured to disobey their Father's warning, two children yield to the seducer and suffer the consequences.
- *Advertising:* Persuaded to give in to their curiosity, two consumers throw caution to the wind and get more than they bargained for.
- *Research:* Deciding to participate in a risky experiment, two investigators test their hypotheses, which produce significant results in advancing their understanding of their environment.
- *Mental state as an extenuating circumstance in law:* Guilty of a capital crime, the Judge "excuses" two criminals by reducing their sentence from death to "imprisonment in life."*

The view that man is *a priori* responsible for his actions is intrinsic to the Jewish and Christian religions. John Milton (1608–1678) was emphatic on this point:

> I formed them free, and free they must remain,
> Till they enthrall themselves: I else must change
> Thir nature, and revoke the high Decree
> Unchangeable, Eternal, which ordained
> Thir freedom; they themselves ordained thir fall.[20]

Indeed, God's incessant punishment of His own creations—the expulsion from the Garden, the Flood, the Confusion of Tongues—makes sense only if human beings are moral agents responsible for their actions. Punishment and forgiveness alike imply and presume personal responsibility. In proportion as we diminish or abolish responsibility, by making it contingent on sanity, we transform our grand religious dramas of retribution and redemption from morality plays into incoherent acts of savage punishment and capricious reward.

---

*Sartre said that man is "condemned to freedom."

The concept of responsibility I embrace here is similar to Kant's, which most modern moral philosophers reject.[21] For example, Bernard Williams, a distinguished professor of philosophy at Cambridge, faults Kant's view of responsibility on the ground that, according to it, "man's capacity to will freely as a rational agent is not dependent on any empirical capacities he may have."[22] Kant's position seems to me correct: The capacity to be a rational agent is essentially an attribution.* Nevertheless, Williams characteristically argues that "there is the obstinate fact that the concept of 'moral agent,' and concepts allied to it such as that of responsibility, do and must have an empirical basis," a basis that Williams situates in the "different degrees of rational control over action." In short, Williams objects to Kant's strict concept of responsibility because it is "based on the proposition that men are beings who are necessarily to some extent conscious of themselves and of the world they live in," which is not true for "the clinical cases of people who are mad or mentally defective."[23] What Williams here advocates, common sense and the law have adopted, lock, stock, and barrel. The result is an inversion of the basic moral values that have prevailed as late as the last century.

- Formerly, good fortune was due to Providence, misfortune to personal misconduct. God was responsible for the person's virtuousness; the individual was responsible for his wickedness.
- Today, good fortune is due to personal effort, misfortune to unfavorable circumstances. The individual is responsible for his successes; racism, sexism, poverty, mental illness (anything but himself) is responsible for his failures.

The notion of personal accountability has thus become virtually obliterated. We no longer regard responsibility as intrinsic to the human actor and his mind. Instead, we regard the individual as intrinsically morally enfeebled, a "machine" equipped with a mind that belongs not to him, but to his brain; a mind whose responsibility is automatically impaired by every real and imaginary impairment of the brain as well as by every real and imaginary "trauma" it suffers.

---

*It is, of course, not completely devoid of empirical content. For example, a sleeping or unconscious person lacks the capacity to be a rational agent; but he also lacks the capacity to be an actor (agent) on the social scene.

Save for athletic contests, few contemporary Americans accept the necessity for the dependable imposition of prescribed penalties for rule-transgression, much less understand the inexorable consequences of failure to adhere to such a policy. It would be impossible to play a game of tennis if the player who hits the ball out of the court would be exempted from penalty if he could convince the umpire that it was not what he intended to do. An observation I offered some years ago is apposite in this connection:

If he who breaks the law is not punished, he who obeys it is cheated. This, and this alone, is why lawbreakers ought to be punished: to authenticate as good, and to encourage as useful, law-abiding behavior. The aim of the criminal law cannot be correction or deterrence; it can only be the maintenance of the legal order.[24]

Absolving the Guilty, Accusing the Innocent

The common-sense assumption that a person is judged to be morally responsible for all of his actions and legally responsible for those that violate the law—but is not judged or held responsible for the actions of others—is false. Actually, a person may be blamed or not blamed for almost anything.[25] As Lise Noel noted: "There is no . . . human situation (such as slavery), no form of persecution (genocide included) for which the oppressor cannot eventually place the responsibility on the shoulders of the victim."[26]

No one likes to be blamed or punished, or feel that he has acted unwisely or wickedly and be tortured by his own conscience. In every age and in every society, people have generated and society has legitimized certain excuses for evading responsibility, by attributing it to causes or agents outside the self. This is not the place for an historical review of making excuses and scapegoating.[27] A few examples should suffice. The Greeks blamed natural catastrophes, such as earthquakes and plagues, on angry gods who could be propitiated by human sacrifice. (The persons chosen as scapegoats were called *pharmakoi*.[28]) The Jews abandoned the practice of human sacrifice and replaced it with the practice of animal sacrifice, blaming and sacrificing goats, hence the term "scapegoat." Other popular scapegoats included astrological influences, demonic possession, women (witches), and Jews ("Christ-killers"). Shakespeare inveighed against the ubiquitous human inclination to project personal responsibility onto agents or agencies outside of the self:

This is the excellent foppery of the world, that when we are sick in fortune, often the surfeits of our own behavior, we make guilty of our disasters the sun, the moon, and the stars; as if we were villains of necessity; fools by heavenly compulsion; knaves, thieves, and treachers [traitors] by spherical predominance; drunkards, liars, and adulterers by an enforced obedience of planetary influence; and all that we are evil in, by a divine thrusting on.[29]

Some human passions may have become domesticated with the advance of civilization, but the passion for scapegoating is not among them. On the contrary. Mistaking it as a combination of morality and science, we practice a virtually limitless existential-legal excusing-plus-scapegoating—attributing the misbehaving person's conduct to child abuse, sex abuse, ignorance, poverty, racism, sexism, bad genes, dangerous drugs, malfunctioning neurotransmitters, and mental illness, that is, to anyone or anything but the agent himself.

In short, we stubbornly deny what we all instinctively realize, namely, that responsibility is a zero-sum game: whatever liability A lacks, loses, or rejects, B possesses, gains, or must shoulder. If, for any reason, one person is not held responsible for his behavior and well-being, others will be held responsible for his behavior or health. This principle is the reverse side of the coin we call "paternalism." In the past, doctors often *imposed* a paternalistic relationship on patients, to dominate and perhaps exploit them. Today, customers often *impute* a paternalistic relationship to vendors, to relieve themselves of responsibility and profit from so doing. This feature now characterizes the relations between smokers and tobacco manufactures, "compulsive" gamblers and casinos, health care customers and the manufacturers of medical devices, parasites with shallow pockets (defined as "victims") and producers with deep pockets (defined as "victimizers").[30] Economically, these policies represent a pseudocapitalist method of redistributing wealth; existentially, they exemplify the infantilization and self-infantilization of one part of the population, and the parentification and self-parentification of another part.

The term "paternalism" has two very different uses. One is to identify an adult's sheltering relationship toward a child who could not survive without such protection. The other is to characterize an adult's ostensibly sheltering but actually stultifying relationship toward another adult who probably could—and should be able to—survive without such protection. Because of this latter usage, we lack adequate terms for describing the relationship between a person who treats the mentally competent Other—or his own self—as a mindless nonagent.* To be sure, the self treating itself as a nonagent and society's acquiescence in the moral evasion it entails—exemplified by the rhetoric of addiction and mental illness—is a relatively recent historical phenomenon. It is therefore not surprising that traditional moral philosophers make no reference to it; but it is surprising that modern moral philosophers ignore it as well.[31]

The thrust of my foregoing remarks is that it is folly to treat moral—personal or political—problems as if they were like mathematical problems. A mathematical problem—for example, calculating the area of a trapezoid—has a solution and, once correctly solved, that is the end of the matter. In contrast, the solution of every personal problem is the source of a new set of problems. For example, the usual solution for a young man's or woman's desire for companionship, sex, and children is marriage and procreation, which creates a new set of problems inexorably associated with matrimony and parenthood. This is why the only definitive solution for the moral problems of the person is his death (or the complete dissolution of his self, such as oriental mystics allegedly seek); and why the only "final" solution for the political problems of society is its dissolution into totalitarian despotism.

Moral problems cannot be solved, they can only be re-solved, by adopting certain principles for coping with the dilemmas they pose. The merit of these principles may then be judged in terms of certain standards, such as evolutionary advantage, religious tradition, ethical principle, or economic, political, and social consequence. After all, a self-disciplined person is, as I noted earlier, simply a person who obeys his inner voice, which is a metaphor for the sum of his value system. Hence, obeying the voice of one's conscience is no better guarantee of right conduct than is obeying the voice of external authority. Many of history's famous despots were well-disciplined persons who probably listened to their own conscience.

Regardless of how zealously we appeal to natural law or religious tradition or some other "higher law," we cannot escape the fact that

---

*The term "therapeutism," used derisively, is gaining currency as a description of this mode of relating.

one man's virtue is another man's vice.* Moreover, not only do different people hold different views about virtue and vice, so do most individuals during different periods of their life. Instead of viewing moral conflict as a "problem" to be solved, we ought to view it as an element inherent in the unfolding of the cultural conversation we call "history," the social conversation we call "human relations," and the self-conversation we call "thinking."

RESPONSIBILITY IN LAW

The words "mind" and "mental" come from the Latin *mens*, which means not only mind but also intention. The Latin *reus* (feminine *rea*), used as an adjective, means both responsible and guilty; as a noun, it means a party to a suit, a (competent) defendant or plaintiff, or a criminal.[32] While the original meanings of these words form no part of American consciousness, the phrase *mens rea*—erroneously translated as "guilty mind," rather than as "responsible mind"—has become incorporated into our legal and psychiatric vocabulary.

The term *mens rea* denotes the mental state of a defendant, typically at the time he committed the offense with which he is charged. In American criminal law, a defendant cannot be found guilty and punished unless he is credited with possessing *mens rea*.[33]** The actual use of this concept may be illustrated by the following hypothetical scenario. Jones kills Smith. The fact that Jones caused Smith's death is not in dispute. However, to convict Jones of being criminally responsible for causing Smith's death, it must be established that, when he killed Smith, Jones possessed *mens rea*. If he did not, then he did not act with criminal intent and his act is not a criminal offense. If Smith's death is judged to be the result of an accident or of (justifiable) self-defense, then Jones is found to be innocent and set free. However, if Smith's death is judged to be due to Jones having killed him while, because of insanity, he lacked *mens rea*, then Jones is declared "not guilty by reason of insanity" (and is incarcerated in a mental hospital until

*This statement should not be mistaken for a defense of so-called moral relativism.

**Persons charged with minor offenses, such as traffic   violations and breaches of civil law are assumed to possess *mens rea*. In such cases, the law does not recognize insanity as an excuse.

he is judged to be sane and no longer "dangerous to himself or others"). In short, Smith's death is attributed either to Jones's sane-free-willing mind or to his insane-incapable-of-willing mind.

As this scenario illustrates, the criminal justice system and the psychiatric institutional system are like Siamese twins; the attempt to separate them is likely to jeopardize the life of one or both twins. Law and the mental health professions share a critical part of our social system, namely, the mechanism for disposing of society's unwanted, by incarcerating, punishing, and (involuntarily) "treating" such persons in prisons, mental hospitals, and forensic psychiatric institutions that formally combine the functions of both.[34] This fact makes the union of law and psychiatry virtually indissoluble.

The Insanity Defense: Medicalizing Mercy

The Latin word *compos* means controlled, as in *compos sui* (self-controlled) and *compos mentis* (controlled mind or sane). For centuries, the notion of *non compos mentis* was used narrowly, to identify individuals incapable of caring for themselves and to appoint guardians over them. Only rarely was it used as an excuse for crime, and then only in cases of murder, to reduce the penalty from execution to life imprisonment. In the late Middle Ages, the use of the excuse increased dramatically as a tactic to mitigate the penalty for suicide, whose frequency also increased dramatically.

Judaism and Christianity both prohibit suicide as self-murder, regarded as an especially heinous type of felonious homicide (*felo de se*). In the fifteenth century, the criminal laws of England combined the ecclesiastical and secular penalties for killing oneself, a development which William Blackstone, the great eighteenth-century English jurist, approvingly summarized as follows:

The law of England wisely and religiously considers that no man has the power to destroy life, but by commission from God, the author of it; and as the suicide is guilty of a double offence, one spiritual, in evading the prerogative of the Almighty, and rushing into His immediate presence uncalled for, the other temporal, against the sovereign, who has an interest in the preservation of all his subjects, the law has therefore ranked this among the highest crimes, making it a peculiar species of felony committed on one's self.[35]

Because suicide was regarded as a double offense, against both God and King, the self-killer was punished doubly, by burying his corpse at the crossroads and by confiscating his worldly goods and bestowing them on the sovereign's Almoner. This savage retribution gradually led English juries—which bore the duty of having to determine the causes of so-called unnatural deaths—to find a way to show mercy to the victims, both dead and alive. They did not have far to look. The method had already been identified by Shakespeare, who, through Hamlet, aptly described it as "making mad the guilty":

> Make mad the guilty, and appall the free,
> Confound the ignorant, and amaze indeed,
> The very faculties of eyes and ears.[36]

Moreover, the Elizabethans had not yet repressed the fact that this was merely a hypocritical strategy:

> . . . What I had done . . .
> I here proclaim was madness.
> Was't Hamlet wronged Laertes? Never Hamlet.
> If Hamlet from himself be ta'en away,
> And when he's not himself does wrong Laertes,
> Then Hamlet does it not . . .
> Who does it then? His madness.[37]

THE WAR ON RESPONSIBILITY

Eighteenth-century England was the most technologically advanced, most prosperous, and most powerful nation in the world. Not by coincidence, Englishmen enjoyed more personal liberty, and killed themselves in greater numbers, than any other people on earth. Under the entry for "self-murder," the *Oxford English Dictionary* offers this example of the use of the word: "1741 . . . 'In such a gloomy, saturnine nation as ours, where Self-murders are more frequent than in all the other Christian World besides.'" However, what was new in England in the eighteenth century was not melancholy but liberty. For the first time in history, the English people began to take seriously the twin ideas of personal freedom and right to property. Recall that, in 1726, after being imprisoned in the Bastille on the basis of a *lettre de cachet*, Voltaire was allowed to go into exile in England. One of his biographers describes him looking out over the Thames "swarming with rich merchant ships . . . surrounded by other barges rowed by men in silk and gold. One glance told him that the rowers were 'free citizens': the joy of liberty and plenty leaped to the eye."[38]

This picture is, of course, too rosy. Still, it is clear that in the cultural climate of the 1700s Englishmen sitting on coroners' juries found the duty of imposing the penalties prescribed by law for suicide increasingly troubling. However, repealing the laws against self-murder was unthinkable. Rulers and ruled alike believed that decriminalizing suicide would be tantamount to sanctioning self-murder, exactly as Americans now believe that "legalizing" drugs would be tantamount to sanctioning drug abuse.[39]

"Insanitizing" Suicide

"Insanitizing" suicide—that is, treating persons guilty of a crime as if they were lunatics—was a perfect, ready-made solution. It allowed English men and women to maintain the religious and legal sanctions against the act and, at the same time, provided a compassionate and seemingly enlightened mechanism for sparing the suicide's family the indignity and economic loss entailed in punishing the deed. S. E. Sprott, a historian of English suicide, summarized this development as follows:

In the eighteenth century, juries increasingly brought in findings of insanity *in order* to save the family from the consequences of a verdict of felony; the number of deaths recorded as "lunatic" grew startlingly in relation to the number recorded as self-murder . . . [B]y the 1760s confiscation of goods seems to have become rare.[40]

It must have been clear to anyone who gave thought to the matter that finding the suicide's "mind" *non compos*—posthumously, exactly at the moment when he was executing his felonious deed—was a legal tactic for circumventing the penalty the law itself prescribed for this crime. Blackstone recognized the subterfuge and warned against it:

But this excuse [of finding the offender to be *non compos mentis*] ought not to be strained to the length to which our coroner's juries are apt to carry it, viz., that every act of suicide is an evidence of insanity; as if every man who acts contrary to reason had no reason at all; for the same argument would prove every other criminal *non compos*, as well as the self-murderer.[41]

The warning was futile and Blackstone probably knew it. The law itself, in all its majesty, defined the jury's posthumous judgment as a genuine finding of fact about the human mind. People need no encouragement to evade responsibility. Yet, here the Law, the Great Teacher, invited just such an evasion. Declaring that suicides were *non compos*, the Law had crafted a mechanism for rejecting responsibility and, aided by the medical profession, wrapped its hypocrisy in the mantle of healing and science. Perhaps this was inevitable. In delicate situations, hypocrisy is often considered preferable to honesty. Such was the case with declaring suicides insane, a policy whose tactical character was not officially acknowledged in the eighteenth century, and has remained officially unacknowledged to this day. Contemporary American society has embraced this legal-psychiatric tactic (of impaired-mental-state-as-an-excuse) and is using it on a scale that Blackstone could never have imagined.*

THE WAR AGAINST RESPONSIBILITY TODAY

As this brief review of the history of the insanity defense demonstrates, the doctrine that suicide is not a deed but the display of a diseased mind antedates not only psychiatry but the modern idea of the mind itself. I maintain that this root image is so intrinsic to the modern idea of mind that ignorance or neglect of it precludes formulating a meaningful account of "the mind."

My suggestion that we treat the concepts of right-and-wrong, responsibility, and mind as a single entity is consistent with the conclusions of many students of the human condition. Remarking on the attractions of causal-deterministic explanations of personal conduct, Isaiah Berlin observed:

To seek to avoid this [the moral categories of right and wrong] is to adopt another moral outlook, not none at all. . . . principally it seems to me to spring from a desire to resign our responsibility, to cease from judging provided we be not judged ourselves and, above all, not be compelled to judge ourselves. . . . This is an image which has often appeared in the

---

*English laws mandating that the suicide be buried at the crossroads and his property be confiscated were repealed only in 1823 and 1870, respectively. Still, suicide was far from being "legalized." Instead of burying the suicide's dead body at the crossroads, the failed or would-be suicide's live body was henceforth buried in the madhouse.

history of mankind. . . . It is one of the great alibis, pleaded by those who cannot or do not wish to face the fact of human responsibility.[42]

The tendency to evade responsibility may be subtly abetted by our vocabulary, that is, by the absence of a verb for "responsibility" corresponding to the verb "liberate." When a person unjustly deprived of liberty is restored to freedom, we say that he has been "liberated." However, when a person unjustly deprived of responsibility—by being declared incompetent to manage his finances or stand trial—is restored to responsibility, we do not say that he has been "responsibilitated," because there is no such word. Instead, we think of such a person also as having been liberated, which is true, since depriving a person of responsibility is one of the most effective ways of depriving him of liberty as well. Nevertheless, liberty and responsibility are not identical; they are two sides of the proverbial coin, each with its distinctive markings.

One of the differences between liberty and responsibility is illustrated by the following observation. The transformation of the child into the adult constitutes (ought to constitute) the paradigm of the process of a person's attaining the benefits and burdens of responsibility. We do not call the result "liberation" (unless we regard childhood as a period of painful unfreedom, which seems to be a relatively uncommon sentiment). We ought to call it "responsibilitation."

Psychiatry, Religion, and Responsibility

The use of insanity in English law dates back to the thirteenth century. However, except as a cover against the crime of suicide, this defense was rarely used before the nineteenth century and hence had little social significance. In the last century, two new powerful social trends converged to change that situation. One trend was the increasing popularity of civil commitment, that is, disposing of certain troublesome family members and minor disturbers of the peace by incarcerating them in madhouses; the other was the increasing popularity of replacing capital punishment by involuntary (mental) hospitalization.[43]

Civil commitment and the insanity defense—the two paradigmatic procedures of psychiatry—resemble and complement one another. Both rest on attributing an absence of *mens rea* to the actor; both result in his loss of liberty in a mental institution; and both function as nuclear weapons in psychiatry's war against responsibility. Because of widespread reliance on these procedures, we live in a social and spiritual atmosphere contaminated with the responsibility-ravaging fallout from the manufacture and use of these weapons of moral mass destruction. There is virtually no interpersonal or social conflict today in which the term "mind" may not be brought into play to evade or mitigate the actor's responsibility for his action. Innocent and guilty actor alike is then deprived of liberty on the ground of nonresponsibility. In effect, we have inverted the Judeo-Christian image of man as *responsible moral agent* and have recast it in the psychiatric image of man as *nonresponsible mental patient*.

The moral revolution that began with the insanitizing of suicide—symbolizing the rejection of responsibility for one of our most fundamental choices in life—was completed, in this century, when the representatives of the Jewish and Christian faiths authenticated the transformation of suicide from sin into sickness. According to *The Encyclopedia of the Jewish Religion*, "Judaism does not consider the individual as the owner or unlimited master of his own life; consequently, suicide, which amounts in rabbinic thought to murder, is strictly forbidden. . . . However, recent rabbinic ruling considers the suicide as being of unsound mind, and as such he is allowed to be interned with others."[44] Christian clergymen follow the same rule. Although those who speak for Judaism and Christianity continue to insist that suicide is prohibited by God, their deeds belie their words. Jewish and Christian clergymen no longer deny religious burial to the suicide's corpse.

Once again in history, the authorities of the sacred and the secular worlds have joined forces, this time in support of the modern West's war against personal responsibility. The combined religious, legal, medical, and popular authentication of the doctrine that people who kill themselves are insane has had far-reaching effects on our society. Like a minute grain of sand stimulating an oyster to form a pearl, this seemingly minor reluctance to confront the moral problem of self-murder stimulated Western society to form the concept of mental illness. If this hypothesis is correct, then the entire scholarly and scientific apparatus that traces the origin of the mind to the soul and equates mind with brain is fundamentally erroneous.*

*The fact that Descartes himself had already corporealized the soul, locating it in the pineal gland, also argues against that genealogy. See chapter 4.

I maintain that the modern idea of the mind derives not from the ancient idea of the soul, but from the Renaissance idea of a "malady" with a special predilection for attacking the minds of self-murderers. During subsequent centuries, this fictitious malady grew steadily more virulent and widespread, with a predilection for attacking the mind of anyone who misbehaves. As more and more (mis)behaviors traditionally attributed to personal choice were attributed to diseases of the mind, mental diseases were attributed to brain diseases, today specifically to "chemical imbalances" causing neurotransmitters to malfunction.

The view that mind and brain are one is not a scientific hypothesis (or fact), as its supporters pretend.[45] Instead, it is a rhetorical ruse concealing our unceasing struggle to control persons by controlling the vocabulary. The language we use to speak about behavior largely determines our position on the issue of responsibility. The discourse of minding implies responsibility. In contrast, the discourse of brain-mind protects us from the dilemmas that the duty of holding ourselves and others responsible entails. It makes no more sense to hold the brain responsible for self-murderous suicide than it does to hold the lung responsible for self-suffocating asthma. That is the analogy we either accept as sophisticated neuroscience, or reject as naive neuromythology.

3

Memory: Fabricating the Past and the Future

This chapter is not intended to be a critical review of what we know and do not know about memory. It is intended to be only a small contribution to our critical understanding of the mind, by examining some common misconceptions and controversies concerning memory.

The word "memory," like the word "mind," is a noun and seems to name an entity that common sense locates in the brain. Lest this idea appear to be convincing, consider a remark of John Albert Macy's (he edited Helen Keller's autobiography). He wrote: "Miss Sullivan says that both she and Miss Keller remember 'in their fingers' what they have said."[1] To a hearing person, this is a seemingly absurd proposition. My thesis is that the proposition that memory is located in the brain is only slightly less absurd. Memory, like mind, is not an entity located in space.

MEMORY: RETRIEVAL, RECONSTRUCTION, CONSTRUCTION

Psychologists tell us that most people "believe without question that past life events are remembered as they actually happened."[2] This view rests on the assumption that our experiences are imprinted on a neural structure, producing a permanent, albeit often inaccessible, "memory trace"; and it is supported by both official and popular science.

Philosopher John R. Searle declares: "When, for example, we *store* memories it seems we must *store* them somehow in the synaptic connections between neurons."[3] A review essay on childhood sexual abuse in the authoritative *New England Journal of Medicine* states: "Clearly, our understanding of memory is crucial to the discussion. Research leads us to consider memory processing as consisting of three stages: 'encoding,' 'storage,' and 'retrieval.'"[4] Finally, in a feature essay in *Newsweek*—captioned "The Cerebral Filing System" and illustrated with a picture of the brain—the reporters explain that "Memories are stored, by category, in different parts of the brain. . . . The job of assembling them falls to a part of the brain called the limbic system. Like a neural file clerk, it [*sic*] pulls disparate aspects of each memory from separate file drawers scattered throughout the cortex, gathering them into a cohesive whole."[5]

None of this is true. To be sure, there are many things we usually remember correctly, especially if they do not concern us personally, such as the capital of New York State or the speed of light. But we tend to misremember the things that affect us personally, such as our past relationships with parents, spouses, and children. None of this is inconsistent with the fact that memory, like the mind, depends on the brain, but is not in it. Our experiences leave an imprint on the brain, as well as on other parts of the body, for example, the immune and the muscular-skeletal systems. However, the belief that memory is a record, a sort of intracranial filing system—and that the relationship between memory and the brain is like the relationship between information in a computer and the disk on which it is stored—is false. B. L. Bugelski, a professor of psychology at the State University of New York in Buffalo, points out that such "language is analogical; the memory of a computer is not like that of a human being. . . . Its 'memory' can . . . be erased completely by one switch setting, without other damage to the computer. Our memories are erased completely only when we are dead."[6]

This is not all. Computer memory is information entered (programmed) into a machine by a human operator; it may be erroneous (because of programmer error or a defective memory chip); it may itself be a lie (assert a falsehood); but "it" cannot lie. In contrast, human memory is what a person recalls or claims to recall: it is an assertion by a person, attributed to his memory; it is intrinsically unreliable, may be unintentionally erroneous, or may be deliberately falsified.

Memory as Human Action

Memory is a matter of *producing* rather than *reproducing*. A recollection is a report, to oneself or others. As such, it is a communication, a form of human action, not the impersonal transfer of an engram from neurochemical processes into "factual information." Because verbalized memory entails the use of language, it entails as well the active participation of the person doing the remembering and speaking.[7]

Memory is not a discrete capacity and remembering is not an isolated act. Virtually everything we do or think partakes of our rememberings, an interpretation consistent with the inability of experimental psychologists and neuroscientists to localize memory in any particular area of the brain.[8] The activity we call "memory" requires the whole brain, because it pertains to the perceptions and behavior of the whole person.

Since reported (verbalized) memory is a type of assertion, our judgment of its validity ought to be measured by the same criteria that govern our judgment of the validity of other assertions. When a recollection is corroborated by authoritative opinion or objective evidence, it is said to be "true." When it is contradicted by authoritative opinion or is inconsistent with objective evidence, it is said to be "false." That is all we can say about the truth or falsehood of any assertion.

Persons engaged in certain professions—archaeologists, anthropologists, geologists, historians, jurists, linguists, paleontologists, and psychiatrists—are especially interested in the past. Why? Ostensibly, because they want to discover what "actually happened," that is, ascertain the so-called "historical truth." In some cases this is largely true (geologists), in others it is largely untrue (trial lawyers). But even when it is largely true, it is not the whole truth. Inexorably, our interest in the past is at least partly strategic, that is, we want to create an account of the past consistent with a *Journalism* certain (preconceived) cognitive or moral scheme. When Michael Oakeshott asserts that "The historian's business is not to discover, to recapture, or even to interpret; it is to create and to construct,"[9] he is exaggerating, but he is saying something important. George Herbert Mead put it thus:

Even the most vivid of memory images may be in error. . . . We are not deciphering a manuscript . . . *[O]ur pasts are always mental in the same manner in which the futures that lie in our imagination ahead of us are mental . . .* they are subject to the same tests of validity to which our hypothetical futures are subject.[10]

One of the decisive differences between animals and human beings is that they live in the present,* whereas we live in the past and the future as well.** The past is important for us because it is our blueprint for the future. We use our memory not only to remember and forget, but also to anticipate and plan. Lewis Carroll phrased this insight as a witticism: "It's a poor sort of memory that only works backwards."[11] (The Queen is speaking to Alice.) Eugene Winograd, a professor of psychology at Emory University, formulates it in academic language. The function of memory, he states, is to provide us "with a sense of continuity about our lives without which it would be hard to conceive of a sense of self. . . . Memory is future-oriented; it prepares the child to act in the world by encoding regularities."[12] This is why severe memory loss is such a devastating deficit. The individual who loses his memory loses his mind, his self, his personhood.

Memory, then, is a narrative we create—and, from time to time, re-create or "correct"—to give permanence and validity to our sense of identity and justify our plans for the future. *Webster's* underscores the personal nature of memory by calling it a "power vested in an individual."[13] Hence, the phrase "personal memory" is a pleonasm, and the phrase "collective memory" is a metaphor. The term "Pearl Harbor" is not merely the memory of an event, but rather the emblem of Japanese treachery and American resolve to avenge it—"a day that will live in infamy," as Roosevelt put it.

Because memory helps us to plan for and shape the future, we often study the past to control the future, for example, in civil and criminal litigation and psychotherapy. Rewriting history, dramatized by Orwell in *Nineteen Eighty-Four*, is not an aberration of totalitarian politics; it is a propensity intrinsic to the human condition. Collectively, we are now actively rewriting our na-

---

*Some animals anticipate the future by means of genetically encoded "habits," such as hibernation and nest-building. Others exhibit non-linguistic behavior that resembles memory and planning, for example, dogs find their way home and apes use implements. However, lacking language, we do not credit them with the ability to "remember" the past or "plan" for the future.

**I am speaking existentially, not biologically. For the young, the future is more important; for the old, the past.

(margin handwritten note: animals Spare pronouns to fit the mind's deficiencies)

tional racial and sexual history, ostensibly in the interests of "social justice." Individually, many people—especially individuals "in therapy" and those engaged in tort litigation—are actively revising their personal history, obviously in their own self-interest.[14]

Memory as Language (Self-conversation)

The connection between language and memory was more obvious in the ancient world, when writing was an esoteric skill and the medium for the acquisition and transmission of knowledge was the spoken word. In those days, as Frances Yates reminds us, "the trained memory was of vital importance. And the ancient memories were trained by an art . . . which we have lost."[15]

Until recently, children were required to memorize long passages—from the Bible, Shakespeare, and so forth—partly to imprint those texts on their minds, and partly to train their memories. Modern reductionist theories of memory ignore the important element of memory-training, partly because they try to explain memory in terms of brain function, and partly because they take for granted our dependence on a technology that subserves modern memory. Without access to paper, pen, pencil, book, blackboard, computer, and so on, the classic Greek orator's success depended largely on his memory. Whereas the modern American politician's success depends largely on his TV personality.

The Greeks viewed training the mind as similar to training the muscles, each process requiring repetition. The orator must talk to himself, repeating certain phrases. The discus-thrower must throw the discus, repeating certain movements. From a fifth-century, B. C., Greek fragment, called the *Dialexeis*, Yates cites the following instruction: "A great and beautiful invention is memory, always useful both for learning and life. . . . [R]epeat again what you hear; for *by often hearing and saying the same thing*, what you have learned comes complete in your memory."[16]

The Greeks' recognition of the importance of self-conversation as an aid to memory was passed on to later generations, repetition-as-inner-dialogue becoming the stock in trade of the mnemonotechnician (teacher of mnemonics). Giovanni di San Gimignano, a renowned medieval preacher, taught that the person who wishes to remember certain phrases "should repeat them with frequent meditation."[17]

The dependence of memory on language is consistent with the fact that we have no memories of our infancy and begin to remember when we begin to talk. As our language-skills develop, our memory improves (and vice versa). At age two, the average child has memory for recent events. By age three or four, he has more complex types of recall, say for food associated with a grandparent (called "generic memory"); or for a visit to the zoo (called "episodic memory"). This developmental process is largely the result of conversations about past events between the child and adults. The child thus learns "the art of shaping events into a story . . . revised as the years pass, with some memories highlighted and others fading to support current views of oneself or emotional preoccupations."[18]

Albeit these formulations are touted as the fruits of recent research, they are but restatements of time-worn insights. Quintilian, a first century A.D. Roman orator, warned: "Every liar had better have a good memory."[19] Mark Twain wisely reminisced: "When I was younger, I could remember anything, whether it happened or not; but I am getting older and soon I shall remember only the latter."[20]*

It is not surprising that we often find it easier to remember things that did not happen than to remember things that did. Persons accused of crimes (and persons accusing others of crimes) are especially adept at remembering falsely. When Colin Ferguson—the black man who shot nineteen white people on the Long Island Railroad in 1994—came to trial, he not only denied that he was the assailant, he "remembered" that the shooter was a white man.[21]

Ardent believers in fashionable foolishness are similarly skilled in remembering things that did not happen. Hollywood celebrities remember their past lives. Noncelebrities, hoping to become celebrities, remember having been abducted by space aliens. A professor of psychiatry at Harvard University Medical School is celebrated, and criticized, for validating the veracity of space abductees.[22] The media report claims of abductions by aliens as if they might be true. *Credo quia absurdum est.*

---

*It is common experience that, by means of repeated self-conversations, we can talk ourselves into or out of almost anything, including remembering things that never happened or forgetting things that did happen.

FORGETTING: LOSS OF MEMORY

We describe people as having a good or bad memory and credit them with special aptitudes and inaptitudes for remembering, say, dates, melodies, numbers, or poems. Clearly, our memory both reflects and shapes who we are: we tend to remember the things that interest us and forget the things that do not.

Let us now turn to the twin phenomena of forgetting and remembering, often described as "losing" and "recovering" our memory. Students of the brain—neurologists and other biological scientists—are interested mainly in memory loss (amnesia, dementia) as an aid to correlating mental functions with brain functions. Students of the mind—psychiatrists and other mental health professionals—are interested mainly in (what appears to be) memory gain (through hypnosis or psychotherapy) as an aid to discovering the causes of psychopathology and a means of curing it. Both enterprises are fraught with many perils, theoretical as well as practical.

One common view of forgetting, which need not long detain us, rests on regarding memory as a container. Once filled, we cannot add to it without discarding some of its contents. As new information enters the mind, old information exits and is "forgotten." This view, which treats forgetting as a passive phenomenon, is inconsistent with many characteristic features of memory, such as remembering things we have apparently forgotten, recognizing that we know something although we cannot recall it ("metamemory"), and remembering things we ostensibly want to forget. It is also inconsistent with the interesting experience called "nostalgia," which is plainly not a part of what was "encoded" about the original event. "We were not feeling nostalgic at the time the remembered experience occurred. Nostalgia has to do with the relationship between the present and the remembered past."[23] I view nostalgia as a particular kind of inner dialogue, consisting of a recollection plus a commentary on it.

The Riddle of Memory's Intracranial Substrate

One need not have any medical expertise to recognize that brain damage is likely to impair the subject's memory. The medical literature is replete with accounts of such cases, one of the most famous being that of a man known as "Mr. M." or "Henry M." or "H. M.".[24]

H. M. was born in 1926 and had an unremarkable childhood. He began to suffer from grand mal seizures in his teens, perhaps the result of a seemingly minor head injury incurred some years earlier. His illness devastated his parents, ruined his education, and finally led to a surgical operation that destroyed him as a person. Unable to tolerate his disability, his parents yielded to the vain hope of a surgical cure for their son's epilepsy. In 1953, Dr. William Beecher Scoville—a charismatic neurosurgeon in Hartford, Connecticut—operated on H. M. The result, he jokingly told his wife, was: "Guess what, I tried to cut out the epilepsy of a patient, but took his memory instead."[25]

In his book on H. M., Philip J. Hilts—a health and science reporter for the *New York Times*—presents a vivid account of this famous patient's story. His descriptions and interpretations, however, are warped by seeing H. M. through the distorting lenses of his destroyers. Here is Hilts's description of the operation:

[T]he young man's awareness of that moment was flushed through the silver tube with his cells. In one sharp intake of air, he lost the world. The abscission of these few organs (chiefly the curled hippocampus and the bundles of tissues leading to it) beneath the brilliant fire of the operating-room light marked both the loss and moment of discovery in the small brick hospital in Hartford, Connecticut.[26]

Nevertheless, Scoville discharged H. M. as "improved." In fact, H. M. was totally destroyed. Hilts writes: "The doctors began to take notes. . . . They stood as explorers at the edge of an impact crater in the fog, trying to feel out the depth and radius of the great hole by hiding out along its edge. The era in which Mr. M. lived, and the medicine of the time, betrayed him."[27] This is just the sort of medical apologetics one might expect from a successful science reporter.

Since his operation, H. M.'s sole function in life has been to serve as an experimental object for generations of neuroscientists. A Harvard researcher calls him "a gold mine, the most famous neurological patient in the world."[28] Although H. M. is often described as a person without memory, this is not true. He remembers many things including how to read, write, and speak and who he is. His I.Q. is unchanged, about ten to twenty points above average. He can recite the Gettysburg Address and name the year that Lincoln took office. However, if he walks from the living room to the bath room, he cannot find his way back. In short, H. M.'s personality is so impaired that he has to be cared for as if he were an infant: "He is utterly dependent upon others. . . . Each morning, Henry would wake up and ask, 'What am I supposed to do now?' His mother often said it was a burden, worse than having a child."[29]

The following observations are particularly relevant to my suggestion that we view mind-memory as self-conversation. Recognizing his inability to recall the simplest fact that he is told, H. M. tries to compensate for this defect by continuously *repeating to himself* the information he wants to retain. "If Henry worked steadily to keep the number [he is asked to remember] before his attention continuously—like batting up a beach ball repeatedly to keep it from hitting the ground—he could remember it. . . . The moment his attention is broken, however, the ball drops and is gone."[30] Actually, we all use this mnemonic device when, for example, we try to remember an address or telephone number while our attention is otherwise occupied.

Hilts describes H. M. as a prisoner of the present, a characterization inconsistent with H. M.'s dreams, some of which clearly hint at his dim recognition of the terrible wrong Scoville did to him.

"Were you dreaming?" [H. M. is asked.]
"Yeah."
"What were you dreaming about?" . . .
"What I could have been . . . I dreamed of being a doctor.
A brain surgeon . . . being successful . . ."[31]

H. M. is not a man without memory. He is the protagonist of Kafka's nightmarish *Metamorphosis* come to life—a man who wakes up one morning to find that he is an insect. Hilts seems to realize that something like this happened to H. M., but his need to exonerate medicine and medical professionals obscures his vision. "The tale of Henry," he concludes, "is the story of the removal of humanity."[32] Hilts recoils from suggesting that it was a physician, ostensibly trying to do good, who was responsible for removing H. M.'s humanity; that physicians—and other medical personnel—continue to exploit H. M.; and that what physicians did to H. M. other physicians continue to do to others—often less radically (with drugs), but in ever-increasing numbers.*

*Hilts views lobotomy as having been a reasonable therapy for mental illness, embraces contemporary coercive psychiatric practices, especially the use of psychotropic drugs, and dreams of a future in which antisocial dispositions, such as the "urge to rape," will be treated with drugs.

"REMEMBERING" FALSELY

The idea that memory is an entity that exists independently of language lies at the root of one of the great "therapeutic" fiascoes of recent times.

Some children with cerebral palsy cannot control the oral muscles necessary for speech and hence cannot speak (normally). However, they can learn to write (with their toes, if necessary), thus demonstrating a capacity for inner speech and a desire to express themselves. There is no evidence for this capacity in autistic children.

Autism is a poorly understood (perhaps genetically caused) condition, manifested by extreme withdrawal from personal contact and virtually absent communication skills. In an effort to establish communication with autistic children, specialists in abnormal child development (mental retardation) assumed that their subjects were capable of communicating and wanted to communicate, but where unable to do so without assistance similar to the assistance enabling children with certain neuromuscular afflictions to communicate. Accordingly, they undertook to "facilitate" their communication.

Facilitated Communication: A Hope Based on a Hoax

Facilitated Communication (FC) is the name of a procedure to help children afflicted with certain neuromuscular disorders, especially cerebral palsy. Developed by Rosemary Crossley, in Melbourne, Australia, in the 1970s, the technique consists of an assistant, called the "facilitator," holding a keyboard of the alphabet in front the subject and bracing his arm and hand, to enable him to spell out the message he wants to convey, but cannot communicate without such assistance. When FC proved to be of value for some children with cerebral palsy, its use was extended to autistic children. The result was a new chapter in the history of the misuse of memory.

Once autistic children were enabled to communicate, one might have expected some to express their gratitude to their devoted parents. That did not happen. Instead, the children began to accuse their parents of sexual abuse. The facilitators unquestioningly accepted the children's claims and reported the parents to the judicial authorities. The authorities accepted the reports as true and set in motion the machinery of the modern state's child-protective agencies. The "abused" child was removed from the home, and the "abusing" parent was arrested, charged, and treated as guilty, exactly as were the victims in Kafka's *Penal Colony*. "My guiding principle," says the officer in charge of that dystopian penal system, "is this: Guilt is never to be doubted."[33]

Some autistic youngsters, without any previous familiarity with the alphabet, composed complex texts. An eight-year-old boy "wrote" a lengthy report of sexual abuse by his mother:

The transcript was more than twenty pages in length and contained correctly spelled, anatomically correct descriptions of oral-genital sex and sodomy. . . . The patient's mother was extremely distressed and expressed suicidal ideation . . . [and] required psychiatric hospitalization. The patient [child] was hospitalized in another psychiatric facility and subsequently placed in foster care. . . . No evidence of physical or sexual abuse was found.[34]

Such feats should have aroused the authorities' suspicions. But they did not. Parents and facilitators alike had a powerful need to believe in the quasi-miraculous power of FC to transform every autistic child into another Helen Keller. When that did not happen, less happy prospects of dramatizations beckoned. The facilitators could indulge themselves by fabricating their own sexual fantasies, attributing them to their autistic subjects, and reaping the rewards of sensational coverage guaranteed by the lurid charges.

A critical look at FC could have alerted any serious observer to the deception and self-deception intrinsic to the procedure. The word "facilitate" implies the presence of a preexisting capacity that is being aided. The term "facilitated communication" prejudges the procedure as a technique that enables a subject to convey information (that he has himself acquired and articulated), if only given an opportunity to do so. The facilitator, in this view, is assumed to function as if he were an inanimate object. In the case of FC, the situation is exactly the opposite of that characteristic of the many instances of impersonally facilitated communication with which we are all familiar.

The impersonal facilitation of human actions—from the simplest to the most complicated—is what technology is all about. Knives and ovens help us to cut and cook food, but they do not tell us what to eat. Telephones and fax machines help us to communicate, but they do not modify the content of our communications. In contrast, "facilitators" are persons, not objects; they can and do influence the content of the subject's communication. Revealingly, the promoters of FC insisted that only individuals who have "bonded" with their subjects can function as facilitators, a clear sign that they function, and are expected to function, as active participants in the communication. The claim that the facilitator simply facilitates the subject's performance is false. It would be more accurate to say that he uses the autistic person's arm as a tool for spelling out his own message, which he then attributes to the subject. The validity of this interpretation was eventually established by appropriate experiments.[35]

In 1992, the spell cast by FC was broken, where it originated. In a case in Melbourne, Australia, brought against the parents of an allegedly sexually abused autistic child, the court ruled—on the basis of irrefutable objective evidence—that "the client [in the case] had demonstrated no capacity for independent communication . . . [and that] all coherent communications . . . had been generated by the assistant [facilitator]."[36] Only then did the parents of the autistic children realize that their dream was a nightmare, and that FC was a "delusionary sham."[37]

There are important lessons in this story about memory as reminding, and about psychiatry as agency-denying.

• Autism and Facilitated Communication: The facilitator disowns his semantic agency and attributes his own voice to the autistic child. The supporters of FC, hoping that autism masks a normal mind, accept the facilitator's rejection of agency and validate his attributing his voice to the subject.

• Schizophrenia and Psychiatry: The hallucinating patient disowns his semantic agency and attributes his own voice to "voices." Psychiatrists, hoping that madness masks a diseased brain, accept the patient's rejection of agency and validate his attributing his voice to Brain Disease.

Paradoxically, the more damning is the evidence against a false psychological theory or phony psychiatric therapy, the more thankless is the task of the critic who exposes the fraud. The public perceives the debunker as a sort of thief which, in a way, he is. He robs the believer of his faith in a power in which he wants desperately to believe. It is of interest to note that the researchers who unmasked FC as a fraud were anxious to exonerate the facilitators, insisting that their findings "demonstrate that the facilitators were *unknowingly* determining what was typed . . . there is no evidence that facilitator influence is purposeful or *intentional*."[38]

This is a pathetic excuse. A person cannot write a coherent report or accusation *unintentionally*. So long as we keep in mind that memory is not a record of past events registered on the mind or the brain, but a narrative that a person constructs with an eye on the future, we can easily avoid being deceived by follies such as Facilitated Communication, False Memory Syndrome, Alien Abduction, and similar crowd madnesses.

MISCONSTRUING MEMORY: "FALSE MEMORY"

"This has been an epic time for false memory," declares Daniel Goleman, who writes on psychology for the *New York Times*.[39] Note the term "false memory," implying that other memories are "true." We are indeed in the midst of an epidemic of persons, mainly children and women, accusing their parents and others of having sexually abused them. Some of the accusers subsequently recant their memories, blame them on their therapists, and are then diagnosed, by other therapists, as suffering from the False Memory Syndrome (FMS). Are the accusers' original claims true? Are their recantations true?

Everyone has recollections that prove to be false, for example, misremembering a telephone number by transposing some of the digits. We do not call such an error a "false memory." We call it "making a mistake." However, when a person misremembers having been sexually abused, accuses an innocent person of the crime, and then recants, we say that she had a "false memory" and suffers from the "false memory syndrome." What is going on here?

As we have seen, a recollection is an assertion that may be true or false, and may be verified or falsified by the observations and testimony of others. Nevertheless, from time to time people treat certain classes of memories—typically of some dramatic wrongdoing or wondrous event—as if they were, *prima facie*, true assertions. Formerly, when religious values formed the basis of the dominant ethic, people tended to accept as true the recollections of individuals who claimed to have witnessed certain women, called witches, copulating with the Devil.[40] Devoutly religious persons still tend to believe the memories of young women who claim to have seen the Virgin.* Today, when health values form the basis of the dominant ethic, people tend to accept as true the recollections of certain persons who call themselves "victims" (of abuse). The practical consequences of such memories are, of course, dramatic, as they are intended to be.[41]

Recovering Lost Memories

Researchers asked groups of people if they believe the following statement about memory: "Everything we learn is permanently stored in the mind, although sometimes particular details are not accessible. With hypnosis or other special techniques these inaccessible details could eventually be recovered." Sixty-nine percent of the general public and 84 percent of those with training in mental health answered Yes.[42]

It is not by coincidence that persons trained in mental health, even more than ordinary people, continue to ignore the self-evident fact that, without corroborating evidence external to an accuser's assertions based on her memory, no observer can confirm or disconfirm the veracity of her assertions.** Jurists, psychiatrists, and the public nevertheless act as if the right thing to do were to accept as valid a woman's accusation of having been sexually abused; and if she recants, as if the right thing to do were to accept as valid her recantation. Belief in this foolishness is facilitated by the image of "false memory" as a sort of computer virus, that a bad therapist/programmer can insert into a mind/program, and a good therapist/programmer can remove from it. This image of the mind as a brain-computer obscures the obvious, namely, that some (perhaps many) accusations of sexual abuse are merely new versions of the ancient sin of bearing false witness.***

*I am not aware of any reports of young men "seeing" the Virgin or of any discussion of why only women report such visions.

**The opposite is not true. In some cases—for example, when the claimant embellishes her accusation by claims of having seen the accused killing children in Satanic rituals—the accusation is, *prima facie*, false. Legal procedures based on the assumption that personal memory is valid and that an accuser's recollection of sexual abuse attributed to a defendant is true make a mockery of the idea of a fair or rational system of justice.

***Exodus 20:16: "Thou shalt not bear false witness against thy neighbor."

The subject of sexual abuse during childhood has a long and ignominious history in psychiatry.[43] One of the reasons is the widely held but false belief that psychiatrists, and only psychiatrists, possess reliable methods for ascertaining whether an event— alleged to have occurred decades ago, in the privacy of a home—has or has not actually occurred. Despite its patent absurdity, this belief remains indestructible. The result is that in the past—when conventional wisdom viewed parents as the paragons of virtue who could do no wrong, struggling to civilize wicked children who could do no right—psychiatrists validated the parents' claims about their children. (They still often do so.) Whereas today—when conventional wisdom defines parents as defective adults and potential sex abusers who can do little that is right, misgoverning innocent children who never lie—psychiatrists validate the (adult) children's claims about their parents.

Regardless of how many allegedly true recollections of abuse memories prove to be false, mental health professionals continue to flood the market with accounts of "recovered true memories" of abuse.[44] A major trade publisher's latest offering promises "Seven spellbinding cases . . . [The author sheds] light on why it is rare for a repressed memory to be wholly false. . . . unforgettable true stories of what happens when people remember what they've tried to forget—plus one case of genuine false memory."[45] The howler, "genuine false memory," has evidently not diminished the credibility or popularity of the book, subtitled, "True Stories of Traumatic Memories, Lost and Found," suggesting that memories, like car keys, can be "lost and found."[46]

Viewing memory as a function of the brain rather than of the person, many neuroscientists and science writers accept the existence of an entity called "false memory." At a Harvard Medical School conference on the subject, there was "scientific agreement on the most likely *neurological and cognitive bases of false memory*. . . . Part of the fragility of memory is due to the way the mind encodes a memory, distributing aspects of the experience over far-flung parts of the brain."[47]

THE FALSE MEMORY SYNDROME: FOLLY SQUARED

False Memory Syndrome (FMS) is the name of a newly minted mental illness. Its reality is actively promoted by the False Memory

Syndrome Foundation (FMSF), a group composed largely of parents who claim they have been falsely accused of sexual abuse as a result of their daughters' therapy.[48] In 1993, the FMSF had more than 4,600 members and their numbers were growing.[49]

What is the FMS? The FMSF defines it as the identification of "a sexually abusive relationship after some decades of amnesia, especially when the memory comes to a mildly disturbed woman in her thirties, enmeshed in therapy with another woman in her thirties, especially if that therapist expresses the belief that sexual abuse in childhood can have serious emotional sequelae unless it is rooted out through various memory-enhancing techniques."[50] This formula fails to acknowledge that so long as a woman in therapy keeps the discovery (realization, possibility) of having been a victim of sexual abuse to herself—that is, if she refrains from blaming others—there can be no FMS. The crucial element in the FMS is not false memory, but false accusation.

I have no desire to exonerate the mountebanks of memory who, under the guise of therapy, meddle in their client's lives. However, having said that, I would like to enter a *caveat*. Let us assume the worst case scenario. A therapist tries to persuade a young woman that her problem—say, a so-called eating disorder—is due to her father having sexually abused her in childhood. This type of interpersonal encounter is not unique. It is similar, for example, to an investment advisor persuading a young heiress to make a certain (bad) investment. In both situations the client is a legally competent adult who seeks the help of an expert and purchases a service that entails requesting and receiving advice. Having received the advice, the client has several options. She can decide to reject the advice, as too risky. She can ponder it, as perhaps sound but requiring further deliberation before taking action. Or she can approve the advice, make it her own choice, act on it, and accept responsibility for the consequences. In other words, a person who recovers memories of sexual abuse—with or without the assistance of a therapist—need not automatically accuse the alleged malefactor of misdeeds. However, if she chooses to do so, and if her charge proves to be false (or if, overcome by guilt, she recants), she ought to be held morally and legally responsible for her behavior.

The point I make here is simple but one I have not seen made in the literature on recovered memories. If we search for something we have lost, a particular goal is implicit (or explicit) in our effort. We look for our car keys, for example, because we want to be able to start our car. Why do young women search for their "lost" memories (of sexual abuse)? To make themselves feel better (which was Freud's aim)? Or to make others (men) feel worse (which is the aim of the radical feminists)? In either case, the finder of the lost memory must take responsibility—and must be held responsible—for what she does with what she finds.

False Memory or Bearing False Witness?

Accusing innocent persons of misdeeds is a practice as old as mankind. The Decalogue brackets bearing false witness with theft and murder, offenses recognized as "punishable in most legal systems of which we have knowledge."[51] This is no longer true. Rarely if ever is a woman who falsely accuses her parents or others of sexual abuse prosecuted for the crime.* Instead, she is treated as a victim of the FMS. If she recovers her false memory of abuse while in therapy, her therapist is likely to be held responsible for the FMS and may be sued for malpractice. Here is an example.

A sixteen-year old girl tells her teacher that she is being sexually abused by her parents. Her mother and father are arrested and charged with the crime. The girl is put in foster care and begins treatment with a female psychiatrist at a university psychiatric clinic. The psychiatrist diagnoses her condition as "post-traumatic stress disorder brought on by sexual abuse." After 100 therapy sessions, the patient tells a judge that she made up the story. The patient and her parents sue the psychiatrist, claiming that she "saw the diagnosis as a certainty and did not check out anything else. . . . She was the *key person* in the entire system." The jury finds the doctor guilty of malpractice and awards substantial money damages to both the patient and her parents.[52] I might add that in this case (and in many others) common sense should have sufficed to impugn the accuser's credibility and prevent this drama from developing. The patient also reported that "her grandmother flew about on a broom . . . that she had borne three children who were killed, and that she had been raped in view of diners in a crowded restaurant."[53]

Clearly, the jury's verdict rested on its accepting the plaintiffs' claim that the "key person" in the case was not the young woman

---

*Before the 1970s, when abortion was a crime, the woman who hired a physician to perform an abortion was similarly not prosecuted.

who bore false witness against her parents, nor the authorities who believed her and acted on her unsubstantiated accusation, but the psychiatrist who treated her as a *bona fide* patient. Judge and jury thus affirmed the popular delusion that a psychiatrist can reliably determine whether a person is lying or telling the truth, and hence that it is the psychiatrist's professional duty to make such a determination. Psychiatrists have themselves to blame for this situation. They have long pretended that they can evaluate their patients' "reality testing" and can determine whether or not a patient is "dangerous to himself or others." When they fail to keep these promises—implicit in the mystique of their social role—they are duly punished, by being found guilty of malpractice.

The following Minnesota case, in which the jury awarded $2.7 million to an adult, *competent* patient (and her husband), is typical. "The lawsuit," brought by Vynnette Hamanne against Diane Bay Humenansky, M.D., "contended that all of Hamanne's recovered memories were false, *implanted* by Humenansky during therapy sessions."[54] The attorney for the plaintiff, who was also a psychologist, argued that "It [implanting false memories versus recovering true memories] is a human rights and civil rights issue in which the patient's legal right to informed consent has been violated."[55]

The booming business of recovering lost memories, true and false, has generated a parasitic business of studying "studies" of the subject and evaluating their "validity."[56]* "Experts" stand ready to support or oppose the claims and counterclaims of everyone in the drama. Most female experts claim that memories of sexual abuse recovered by women are always, or almost always, true. The authors of the popular *The Courage to Heal* recommend that women try to retrieve and trust their memories of sexual abuse: "If you think you were abused and your life shows the symptoms [*sic*], then you were."[57] A (female) Harvard psychiatrist asserts: "False claims of childhood sexual abuse are demonstrably rare. . . . To fasten upon false memory as the main event is far-fetched and bizarre."[58] Another (female) expert advises that, in the absence of direct evidence of abuse, we must rely "on indirect corroborative evi-

---

*This is largely a female business. Virtually all the mental health experts who help women recover lost memories of sexual abuse as well as most of those who testify in lawsuits claiming that the women's therapists have negligently implanted false memories in their minds are women.

dence . . . [such as] a diagnosis of post-traumatic stress disorder having no other apparent cause."[59] Talk-show hostess Sally Jesse Raphael states: "I personally have never met anyone who lied about being an incest victim."[60] Female practitioners featured on a PBS television "Frontline" TV series assert that "they are convinced by the emotions of their clients. . . . 'When they access a memory, they are doing it out of what's coming up from within them, and the body doesn't lie nor does the psyche.'"[61]

The reasoning of the critics of the memory-recovery business, many of whom are men, is not much more rigorous. They maintain that memories recovered in therapy are usually false; debunk the "myth of repressed memory";[62] and warn that "recovered memory therapy . . . may be hazardous to the patient's health."[63]

There are many reasons why people fabricate false memories: because dramatic accusations, especially of sexual wrongdoing, attract attention and are sources of fame and money; because revenge is sweet; because people have a need to explain their unexplained emotional distress, the greater the distress, the greater the need for a spectacular "cause"; because human beings have a penchant for attributing their evil impulses to Others; and because, as I noted, psychiatrists stand ready to relieve people of responsibility for their behavior—including the responsibility to verify, for themselves, whether others are telling the truth or not.

The scandal of the FMS illustrates the danger of confusing a strategic prejudgment with the ostensible description of a phenomenon. Labeling a libelous accusation the False Memory Syndrome implies that "normal" memory is true; that a "false memory," even if it is advanced as a malicious accusation, is the symptom of a mental illness; and that the person who engages in bearing false witness is not sinning but sick, the victim of a disease that causes her to remember falsely and charge innocent individuals with serious crimes.

Suicide, homosexuality, masturbation, and bearing false witness are among the sins prohibited in the Bible. The first three have already passed through the purifying metamorphosis from sin into sickness, homosexuality advancing to normal life style, and masturbation graduating to therapy. Bearing false witness has joined this parade.

The Experts Speak

By 1994, the problem of ascertaining the validity of memories recovered during therapy became so pressing that medical and mental health organizations felt it necessary to issue guidelines concerning the subject. The American Medical Association's (AMA) preliminary report begins with the gauche statement that "false memories can develop,"[64] as if memories developed like lesions, instead of being designed by persons. Then, by means of continual references to the brain, the report depersonalizes and exonerates the bearers of false witness. "The way information is stored," the AMA declares, "is a function of what part of the brain is on, and the way it gets recalled is also a function of what part of the brain is on."[65] This description makes it seem as if the brain were like a television set, the content of "its" recollections determined by the channel to which it is tuned. The report ends with the following remarkable assertion by Charles R. Marmar, M.D., president of the International Society for Traumatic Stress Studies at the University of California in San Francisco: "But there will be no 'true test' of whether memories are true or false until we have really much more sophisticated *biological* measures."[66] Evidently, the experts are still looking for a "truth serum"—this time not a sedative like a barbiturate, injected into the patient, but a substance in the patient, like a neurotransmitter: That, they hope, would furnish us a "true test" of whether a person is telling the truth or lying.

The American Psychological Association's guidelines concerning false memories are not much better. The Association's experts declare: "Research indicates that some individuals who 'recover' memories of being abused as children have constructed so-called pseudomemories, though studies have yet to explain the *process by which these pseudomemories develop.*"[67] Lies are lies, not "pseudomemories." We know why people lie and do not need "studies" to explain it. Fatuously, the panel concludes: " 'Repressed memories' of childhood sexual abuse that are recovered years later should not all be taken at face value but should not all be dismissed. . . . It is . . . possible to construct convincing pseudo-memories for events that never occurred."[68]

Covering all bases, the American Psychiatric Association's report concerning recovered memories of childhood sexual abuse warns of the "risks of dismissing true accounts or believing false ones."[69]

Leading psychiatrists carefully refrain from raising questions about fundamental issues at stake. Instead, they attribute the problems of recovering repressed memories to "abuses" by ignorant practitioners. Walter Reich, a psychiatrist at the Woodrow Wilson International Center for Scholars in Washington, writes: "Probably the main reason for the growth of *false* charges of abuse has been the recent proliferation of abuse specialists and therapists, many of whom lack any knowledge of mental illness or the workings of memory."[70] This interpretation flies in the face of the fact that Freud—the Galileo of the "workings of memory"—was a pioneer enthusiast of repressed memories recovered with the aid of hypnosis and psychoanalysis.

THE BURDEN OF FREUD'S LEGACY

Although Freud's keen interest in the nature of memory is familiar to psychiatrists and educated lay persons, many authors who now address the subject ignore his work. I shall briefly show that the currently fashionable fallacies concerning recovered memories have their roots in Freud's writings.

Hysteria and Repression

Freud was obsessed with what he called "repressed" memories, exemplified by infantile sexuality and the Oedipus complex.[71] He used the term "repression" for the first time in *Studies in Hysteria* [1893–1895], where he described it as an intentional act: "[it] was a question of things which the patient wished to forget, and therefore *intentionally* repressed from his conscious thought and inhibited and suppressed."[72] A few years later, he wrote: "Half the secret of hysterical amnesia is uncovered when we say that hysterical people do not know what they do not want to know."[73]

It must be emphasized that, in writing about memory, Freud usually considered the subject in terms of "amnesia" (a real or alleged condition), rather than in terms of forgetting and remembering (actions). The following excerpt is typical: "[A] normally developed child of three or four already exhibits an enormous amount of highly organized mental functioning . . . there is no obvious reason why *amnesia* should overtake these psychical acts."[74] The Latin word "amnesia" has powerful neurological-pathological overtones. The term "infantile amnesia," which resonates with the term "infantile paralysis," pathologizes normal childhood. Freud thus explains the ubiquitous phenomenon of not remembering early childhood experiences by pathologizing it and then offering the mythology of an Oedipus complex as its ostensible cause. A simpler and more plausible explanation is that such experiences are forgotten because the child possesses only rudimentary verbal skills and because the events do not have a lasting interest for him and he therefore does not keep talking about them. As Ulric Neisser, a professor of psychology at Emory University, wisely remarks: "You don't see a bunch of three-year-olds sitting around talking about old times."[75]

Freud's linkage of forgetting and sex is implausible, to say the least, since adults have no memories of *anything* that happened during their early years. It is also worth noting that the "Index" to the *Standard Edition* lists hypnotic amnesia, hysterical amnesia, infantile amnesia, and traumatic amnesia, but does not list senile amnesia, the commonest form of forgetfulness. Could this omission be due to the fact that this is the only type of amnesia Freud could not possibly attribute to sexuality?

Through his long career, Freud never relinquished his materialistic, quasi-neurological conception of memory. Early on, he described memory "as an archive open to anyone who is curious." However, not everything *in* the archive is available for the reader because some of the material "is subject to restriction by a trend of the [subject's] will."[76] At the end of his life, returning to one of his favorite analogies—between the buried ruins archaeologists study and the "buried" memories psychoanalysts study—Freud remarked: "Indeed, it may, as we know, be doubted whether any psychical structure can really be the victim of total destruction."[77] Here the metaphor becomes literalized and we are asked to believe the absurdity that our mind/brain houses indestructible "psychical structures."

This materialist-mechanist view of remembering led Freud to treat memories as if they were like microbes, which could become "pathogenic" and cause illness, specifically, "hysteria." In 1893, he wrote: "We find two groups of conditions under which memories become pathogenic. . . . the subject may simply refuse to react, may not *want* to react to the psychical trauma."[78] In 1894, he added: "[T]his kind of 'forgetting' did not succeed with the patients I analyzed, but led to various pathological reactions."[79]

Next, Freud seized on the idea that to become pathogenic, the memory must be of a sexual nature: "This [pathogenic] agent is indeed a memory relating to sexual life. . . . One only succeeds in awakening the psychical trace of a precocious sexual event under the most *energetic pressure of the analytic procedure*, and against an enormous resistance. Moreover, the memory must be extracted from them [patients] piece by piece."[80] The spectacle of Freud extracting memories, like a dentist extracts an impacted molar, makes current accounts of therapists trying to recover repressed memories look tame in comparison.

In 1896—only three years after acknowledging that he was "extracting" memories from his patients—Freud began to consider the problem of "false memories." Pretending to be innocent of the offense he had himself created, Freud warned: "One must beware of *forcing on patients supposed reminiscences* of this kind by questioning them. . . . no one should form too certain judgments in this obscure field until he has use of the *only method* which can throw light on it—of psychoanalysis for the purpose of making conscious what has so far been unconscious."[81] This claim is at once arrogant and disingenuous. Freud was too intelligent not to recognize that without access to other informants and other information, there is no method by means of which we can reliably confirm or disconfirm the veracity of a person's recollections of his or her childhood sexual experiences. Nevertheless, he boldly offers psychoanalysis as a kind of non-pharmacological truth serum that enables the analyst to overcome the patient's resistances and thus discover his secrets, hidden even from himself. To believe this tale, one must be gullible indeed.

Finally, in 1909, Freud offered this often quoted statement about the origin and nature of hysteria:

[O]ur hysterical patients suffer from reminiscences. Their symptoms are residues and mnemic symbols of particular (traumatic) experiences. . . . The monuments and memorials with which large cities are adorned are also mnemic symbols. . . . These monuments, then, resemble hysterical symptoms in being mnemic symbols.[82]

Freud's analogy between the hysteric's traumatic memories and a nation's historic monuments is singularly inept. People do not erect monuments to military heroes who protected them from their enemies in order to suffer every time they look at them. Yet, Freud says that hysterics suffer from memories that resemble such monuments. He was 180 degrees off the mark. People erect historic monuments to admire heroic persons and heroic deeds.

Hysterics, Freud continued, "cannot get free of the past and for its sake they neglect what is real and immediate. This fixation of mental life to pathogenic traumas is one of the most significant and practically important characteristics of neurosis."[83] Again, Freud has it exactly backwards. Hysterics are unwilling, not unable, to free themselves of their past; they are sickened by what they see in their future, not their past.*

Hysteria and Revenge

Freud's observations support the interpretation that hysterics suffer not from traumatic reminiscences but from frustrated desires for revenge.** In the first chapter of *Studies on Hysteria*, written jointly with Breuer, Freud explicitly identified revenge as the hysteric's aim: "The injured person's reaction to the trauma only exercises a completely 'cathartic' effect if it is an *adequate* reaction—as, for instance, revenge."[84] Consistent with this understanding, he conceptualized his treatment as talking the patient out of her motives for revenge: "[I] insisted on her continuing her story till the pain had been talked away. . . . I used to say, half-jokingly, that I was talking away a certain amount of her motives for pain."[85]

On at least two other occasions Freud acknowledged the role of revenge as a motive for mental illness. In 1920, in his paper on female homosexuality, he wrote: "She [the patient] *wanted* her father to know occasionally of her relations with the lady, otherwise she would be deprived of the satisfaction of her keenest desire—namely, revenge."[86] And in 1925, he offered this remark about Hamlet: "It could scarcely be a chance that this neurotic creation of the poet should have come to grief, like his numberless fellows in the real world, over the Oedipus complex. For Hamlet was faced with the *task of taking vengeance* on another for the two deeds which are the subject of the Oedipus desires."[87]***

---

*The life history of Bertha Pappenheim ("Anna O.") is illustrative.

**I use the term "hysterics" to refer here mainly to persons so characterized by Freud.

***A person who discovers that his mother and uncle have conspired to kill his father has a reasonable, real-life motive for revenge. Nevertheless, to buttress his own theories, Freud attributed Hamlet's behavior to his Oedipus complex. I have addressed Freud's distortion of the Oedipus legend and his own life-long lust for revenge in *The Myth of Psychotherapy*.

These passages, together with careful reading of Freud's other writings reveal that he realized that remembering is a kind of internal dialogue, created and re-created by the subject. In 1895, Freud wrote: "[Fräulein Elisabeth von R.'s] painful legs began to 'join in the conversation.' . . . While we are working at one of these [hysterical] symptoms we come across the interesting and not undesired phenomenon of 'joining in the conversation.' The problematical symptom re-appears."[88] A year later, he restated this observation as follows: "During this work of reproduction [of memories], the physical sensation in her abdomen 'joined in the conversation' as it were, as is regularly observed to happen in the analysis of hysterical mnemic residues."[89] Note that Freud here refers to mental symptoms as *voices* or *speakers* that participate in the dialogue between therapist and patient. However, because Freud wanted to construct a structural, not a semantic, theory of mind/memory, he ignored his own observations.

Freud's mistakes continue to confuse our understanding of memory. Although he correctly maintained that loss of memory is often the result of motivated action (repression), he failed to see that so is the recovery of memory (remembering). Unconverted into dialogue, autologue keeps the hurts received and the harms unresolved alive. So-called repressed memories are remembered because the subject continually reminds himself of them. Aptly, we speak of a person "nursing" his grievances. Relinquishing such "nursing"—in the religious confessional or in secular psychotherapy—drains it of affect and interest and thus dissipates it.

His references to revenge notwithstanding, Freud failed to distinguish between two radically different motives for "recovering" and remembering traumatic memories, namely, to avoid future harms and to avenge past injuries. This failure is probably due to his particular motive for wanting to recover buried traumatic memories: He wanted his patients to "remember" to enable them to master their misery by, as it were, forgiving and forgetting their past victimization (a process he called "treating neurosis"). As a result, he neglected revenge as a morally legitimate (albeit perhaps ignoble) tactic for healing the wounds of victimization. In this respect, the feminists' objections to Freud are fully justified. Albeit the feminists' motive for wanting women to recover buried traumatic memories is also "therapeutic," their quest rests on the assumption that the subjects' victimization in the past is an emblem for their continuing victimization in the present and that the only effective means for remedying these injuries is by means of retaliatory-litigious counteraggression.

In short, Freud wanted the "neurotic" to master her past trauma internally, by what he called "working through"; whereas feminists want the "victim" to master it externally, by legal and social action. Freud is thus innocent of the retaliatory use of recovered-invented "memories." Therein also lies his guilt.

REVENGE AS REMEMBRANCE

The word "vengeance" comes from the Latin *vindicare*, which means "to vindicate." Situated in the context of a prior act of invalidation, vengeance is the ultimate act of self-validation. A person cannot vindicate himself unless he has been wronged, typically by others.

Less often, injury to the self is self-inflicted, by doing injustice to others. Such a person may seek expiation by self-injury. However, if the injury to the self is inflicted by others—by prejudice, false accusation, or unjust punishment—then the experience of wronged innocence is likely to engender revenge against the guilty parties. The popularity of books such as Emily Brontë's *Wuthering Heights* or Alexandre Dumas's *The Count of Monte Cristo* testifies to the importance of this motif as an act of mental self-repair. Communities feeling wronged and planning revenge are engaged in similar acts of collective self-repair and self-vindication. Herein lies the source of many of the cycles of ethnic and religious wars that characterize much of what we call "history."[90]*

Vengeance: Divine and Human

Revenge and forgiveness are some of our most important motives and actions; they are also some of the most important attributes of the gods we create in our own image. Jehovah is the deified incarnation of revenge: "Vengeance is mine."[91]** Jesus is

---

*The behavior of some feminists and mental patients is similarly motivated by revenge against their actual or perceived oppressors. Others, especially unhappy children, may injure or threaten to injure themselves, in an effort to control their adversaries by making them feel guilty and remorseful.

**Mortal man is unable to observe this injunction. The thirst for revenge is a basic human passion that, like other passions, must be tamed.

the deified incarnation of mercy: "But that ye may know the Son of man hath power on earth to forgive sins."[92]

The rabbi lacks the power to forgive. For the Jew who sins, salvation depends neither on repentance-and-pardon, nor on God's grace, but on his own conduct.[93]* He must atone for his transgressions, an act epitomized by the celebration of the Day of Atonement (*Yom Kippur*): He must pray, abstain from food and drink, and seek the pardon of his fellow men whom he has wronged during the past year. The ritual ends with the sacrifice of a goat, upon whom the sinner casts his sins.[94] "And Aaron shall lay both his hands upon the head of the live goat, and confess over him all the iniquities of the children of Israel, and all their transgressions in all their sins, putting them upon the head of the goat, and shall send him away by the hand of a fit man, into the wilderness."[95]

The Christianization of Judaism softened these harsh demands by offering absolution from sins through repentance, confession, and even ignorance, the latter excuse epitomized by Jesus's words on the cross: "Then said Jesus, Father, forgive them; for they know not what they do."[96] Unlike the Old Testament, the New is replete with references to forgiveness. God is now specifically identified as the incarnation of this virtue: "To the Lord our God belong mercies and forgiveness."[97]

Because we cannot live without self-esteem, we long to have our sins forgiven and avenge the wrongs done to us. By forgiving us, the Other validates us. By avenging ourselves, we validate ourselves. The final act in the religious drama of human life is the Last Judgment, rendered by God. We want to reserve both Forgiveness and Vengeance to God, letting him render the Final Exoneration or Final Condemnation. He must have the Last Word. The agnostic, however, believes that forgiveness and revenge are, to paraphrase Talleyrand, too important to be left to God. Both are essential elements in personal self-development and social relations. As the body heals injury to its integrity by replacing the damaged part or forming scar tissue, the self heals injury to its integrity by forgiveness and revenge. Both acts dissipate the trauma of traumatic memories.

---

*For the same reasons, non-Jews can enter the Jewish heaven, provided they have not violated the Laws of Noah. These laws—that, according to the Talmud, all human beings, not only Jews, must observe—include prohibitions against blasphemy, bloodshed, idolatry, and robbery and the precept to practice equity.

4

Brain: The Abuse of Neuroscience

In 1993, Bill Moyers presented an acclaimed series of television broadcasts on how "the mind heals the body." In an interview, he explained: "I looked into an open skull during brain surgery. I thought, 'I can see the brain, but where's the mind?'"[1] Moyers' puzzlement illustrates how well his ear is tuned to asking the politically and scientifically correct question, to which there is now only one proper answer: Mind is *in* the brain; or, better, mind *is* the brain.

Although equating mind with brain implies a denial of the distinctively human activities called "minding," "talking to oneself," and "being responsible," many experts now support this view.[2]* "[T]he brain and mind are one," declares Alan J. Hobson, professor of psychiatry at Harvard. "They are one entity. . . . I use the hyphenated term 'brain-mind' to denote unity. . . . Every detail of a dream can be accounted for in terms of neuronal signal-patterns."[3]

Daniel C. Dennett, professor of philosophy at Tufts University, puts it more succinctly: "The mind is the brain."[4] Why, then, do we have two words for it? Because mind does not mean brain. Indeed, Dennett himself uses the word "mind" to refer to a nonexistent "inner sanctum that science cannot reach."[5] British novelist and

---

*Freud's work intself stands as a massive speculation about the mind as a (quasi)-biological entity, which he called the "mental apparatus" and located in the brain.

science writer John Cornwell summarizes Dennett's thesis thus: "Forget the inner life . . . get rid of the self* . . . 'gift,' 'giftedness,' and 'responsibility' are banished from the vocabulary."[6] Dennett does not consider the possibility that mind is minding.

To put to rest any lingering doubts about the unity of mind and brain, some of the most prestigious American universities have established institutions embodying the phrase "mind-brain": Harvard University has launched a "Mind/Brain Institute."[7]

Explanations of mind-as-brain—especially if they are accompanied by alleged documentation couched in terms unintelligible to the layman—are guaranteed to elicit the awed approval of the press and the amazed admiration of the public. The materialist is, of course, partly right: There can be no self or thought without a material substrate. But he is fundamentally mistaken: There can be no materialist account of language, much less of human existence as personal experience.

A NEW SCIENCE OF THE MIND?

During the past few decades, professionals from many different disciplines have published popular books offering materialist explanations of the mind. Although the authors differ in their professional background, all seek to explain the mind in terms of the brain. None treats the person as a responsible, moral agent.

The mathematicians, neuroscientists, and philosophers who offer these seemingly supersophisticated accounts of the relationship between mind and brain claim that they are laying the foundations of a new science of the mind. Perhaps so. I doubt it. I believe they are writing science fiction or are justifying the medical (psychiatric) control of deviance or both. Nevertheless, these new tales of neuromythology mesmerize the public, and perhaps the mythologizers themselves. Why? Because the writers illustrate their stories with striking images of the brain obtained by high-tech scanners, analogize and equate the mind with the brain, use incomprehensible mathematical symbols or give ordinary terms novel, idiosyn-

---

*This injunction strikes me as particularly disingenuous and offensive. It is one thing for a Buddhist monk—who renounces family and property—to reject the clamorous claims of selfhood. It is a very different thing for an American academic—who brazenly seeks self-gratification—to counsel rejecting the self.

cratic meanings, and promise to bring closer a brave new world of Mental Health.

The Neurophilosopher: Agent of the Therapeutic State

The principal interest of a scientist is supposed to be discovering "how things work," not curing AIDS or building a better society. Developing treatments for diseases is a matter of applied science; drafting programs for improving society is a matter of politics.

Most contemporary philosophers of the mind dabble in (what they view as) neuroscience and present themselves as biologically sophisticated, scientific thinkers. To contrast them with moral philosophers, I call them "neurophilosophers" and "biological philosophers." However, their professional identification obscures their true agenda, which is social betterment, as they see "betterment." For Dennett, it is destroying religion and responsibility: He calls religions "infections" and asserts that "Safety demands that religions be put in cages."[8] For most of the other biological philosophers, betterment is helping to win the war against mental illness. A cover story in *Time* magazine offers this typical hype: "Until just a few years ago, unravelling the relationship of mind and brain was beyond the realm of observation and experimentation. . . . As neurologists, psychologists, and biologists have zeroed in more and more on the physical causes of mental disorders, they have found themselves addressing a much deeper mystery. . . . What precisely is the mind? . . . Science can now answer this age-old question. . . [it] has finally begun to catch up with philosophy."[9] The concluding assertion rests on a fundamental fallacy. Science can never catch up with philosophy, because philosophers do not ask the sorts of questions scientists can answer. However, philosophers can catch up with pseudoscientists and mental health propagandists, which is what many neurophilosophers have done.

"What is so exciting," says Patricia Churchland, a professor of philosophy at the University of California in San Diego, "is that philosophical questions raised by the Greeks are coming within the province of science. . . . [We now have] an enormous opportunity . . . to understand and treat such devastating mind malfunctions as . . . depression, drug addiction, schizophrenia."[10] For a detailed exposition of the glories of such a scientific philosophy of the mind, we must turn to the work of Patricia Churchland's husband.

Paul Churchland, also a professor of philosophy at the University of California in San Diego, pulls no punches about his commitment to a reductive-materialist view of the human mind. In his latest book, *The Engine of Reason, the Seat of the Soul*, he asserts that all human mental life is reducible to the brain viewed as a "biological computer."[11] By giving his book the subtitle, "A Philosophical Journey Into the Brain," Churchland implies that it is possible to undertake a meaningful "philosophical journey" into a bodily organ. To impart sense to this absurd metaphor, he systematically replaces statements about actors and actions with statements about brains and neurological pathways. The following formulation is typical: "Any peach, at a comparable step of maturity, will produce almost exactly the same pattern of [neuronal] activation. . . . the subjective taste just *is* the activation pattern across the four types of tongue receptors."[12] Churchland belabors this old-fashioned psychophysical parallelism as if it were a new neurophilosophical discovery and as if it constituted evidence for the validity of prevailing psychiatric theories and practices.

After filling hundreds of pages with words and pictures about brains, computers, synapses, neural pathways, and other elements of fashionable neuromythological discourse, Churchland demonstrates that the bottom line of the "new science of the mind" is, for him also, better psychiatric control of society's unwanted. "Mental illnesses such as schizophrenia," he writes, "may arise from characteristic chemical disorders in the neurochemical environment of the brain's 10 to the 14th power synapses. This assumption suggests a line of treatment or control for the major forms of mental illness."[13] Fearing that he has gone too far in unmasking himself, Churchland offers this disclaimer: "I may seem to be arguing here in favor of a wholesale replacement of talk therapies with chemical, surgical, and genetic therapies. That is not my purpose."[14] However, that is precisely the thrust of his argument, as his following statement—surely astonishing for a professor of philosophy to assert—illustrates: "The social institution of language has nothing to do with the genesis of consciousness."[15]

Actually, Churchland's views on mental illness are indistinguishable from the views of mental health propagandists. "The discovery of chlorpromazine," he explains, "transformed the nature of psychiatric care in North America. . . . Within two decades of its discovery, our many 'insane asylums' [sic] were largely emptied."[16] For evidence that depression and elation are diseases, he offers the observation that "Winston Churchill was certainly thus afflicted to some degree, as, less certainly, was Mozart. . . . All we can be *sure* of is the *presumptively* neurochemical nature of both afflictions [i.e., unipolar and bipolar illnesses.]"[17] How anyone can be *sure* of the *presumptive* cause of a putative illness, and what all this has to do with philosophy, are mysteries that further neurophilosophical research will no doubt dispel.

In the concluding chapter of his book, titled "Neurotechnology and Human Life," Churchland assures us that "A neurally informed and technologically sophisticated society will be able to make judgments reliably and do things effectively."[18] Why? Because "The new scanning techniques will allow us to accumulate a large data base concerning individual profiles of brain functions from normals through violent sociopaths. . . . A large number of such sets will constitute a training set for the sort of diagnostic network we desire, a network that, once trained, . . . will accurately predict problematic social behavior."[19] Experts in neurotechnology will then be able to make a "detailed sociopathic diagnosis" and offer "recommendations about possible treatments. . . . If only half of our *convicts* could be deflected from prison in this way (through neurotechnology], *maintained by cheap pharmaceutical implants, voluntarily received*, we would save billions of dollars in direct cost each year."[20] Concerns about psychiatric abuses Churchland dismisses with this analogy between depression and diabetes:

[G]ood and responsible people in psychiatric and neurological medicine . . . try to restore neural cognitive and emotional function to people who have lost it through illness. . . . There is nothing sinister here. . . . Giving a serotonin-enhancing drug for major depression is no different from giving insulin for diabetes to compensate for a shortfall in natural insulin. . . . The brain is a physical organ like any other, and it may occasionally need some benign medical intervention like any other.[21]

The reader must decide whether this passage betokens political naivete, self-deception, ideological bias, bad faith, or invincible ignorance. Whatever the answer, Churchland's style suggests that he is unfamiliar with the language and concerns of moral philosophy. For example, he seems to think that the term "moral agent"— which he capitalizes—refers to a person conventionally regarded as "moral." He writes: "The common picture of the Moral Agent as one who has acquiesced in a set of explicit rules, imposed from the outside—from God, perhaps, or from Society—is dubious in the extreme."[22]

Churchland's moral-philosophical nescience—a curious fact about a professor of philosophy—may account for the way he ends his book. Evidently still unsure of the validity of his basic thesis, Churchland sets up a straw man and knocks him down. The straw man is the idea of self-knowledge, cast in the phrase, "the mind knows itself." This proposition, Churchland triumphantly announces, "cannot possibly be true. For it amounts to the claim that neural networks have automatic and certain knowledge of their own cognitive abilities. And this claim is simply false."[23] To my knowledge, no one has ever claimed that *neural networks* know themselves. To be sure, an ancient philosopher—no doubt also suffering from a mental illness Churchland could confidently diagnose—did suggest that the unexamined life is not worth living; and since then, many others—no doubt thoughtlessly—have entertained the idea that a *person* can know himself (just as he can know others and the world about him). But Churchland seems blind to the reality of persons. For him, knowledge is an attribute of neural networks.

Churchland's finale is truly mind/brain boggling. "The aim of these concluding suggestions," he declares, "is not to deny us our humanity, but to see it better served than ever before. That is why understanding the brain is so supremely important. It is the engine of reason. *It is the seat of the soul.*"[24] With this sentence, on page 319, the book ends. Three-hundred ten pages earlier, Churchland asserts: "The doctrine of an immaterial soul looks, to put it frankly, like just another myth, false not just at the edges, but to the core." So is soul a myth or is "it" in the brain?

Who cares about linguistic precision or, for that matter, the truth, when he is engaged in waging a holy war on mental illness?[25] We possess a wondrous neurotechnology and leading researchers in our leading institutions are eager to use it. Investigators at the Harvard Medical School and the National Institute of Mental Health have conducted an "automated telephone screening survey for depression . . . [using] computerized digital voice recordings and touch-tone responses to assess symptoms of depression." Reporting their findings in the *Journal of the American Medical Association*, the mental health experts concluded that this "readily available, low-cost technology provided a fully automated . . . method of screening for a common mental illness . . . [which revealed that] the 70.6 percent rate of positivity for depression among participants . . . is similar to the average rate of 76.6 percent found at all in-person National Depression Screening Day sites in 1993."[26]

MIND AS CONSCIOUSNESS

While the Churchlands' neurophilosophy is patently naive, the writings of the more sophisticated practitioners of this new cult thrust in the same direction. They do so, in the main, by substituting consciousness for mind and offering recondite pseudobiological speculations about "it." But what is consciousness? It is an elusive concept about which Hughlings Jackson, the great nineteenth-century British neurologist, had this to say: "There is no such entity as consciousness; we are from moment to moment differently conscious. . . . [consciousness is] the directional mechanism of attention."[27] Focusing on the relationship between language and (human) consciousness, George Steiner offers this penetrating insight: "Psychoanalysis is, *in toto*, a language art, a language *praxis*. . . . Human consciousness is 'scripted' and made intelligible by semantic decipherment."[28] If Jackson and Steiner are right—and I am confident they are—then there is no "consciousness" (as a unitary event or experience) to explain. There is only *human minding*, that is, attending to the ever-changing aspects of our environment (including our self) and articulating as well as deciphering the experience *as* and *in* "language" (self-conversation).

Consciousness as a Property of the Brain

The leading practitioner of philosophizing based on reducing mind to consciousness and consciousness to the brain is John R. Searle, professor of philosophy at the University of California at Berkeley. Describing himself as an "antireductionist materialist," he states: "Consciousness is a mental, and *therefore* physical, property of the brain."[29] His review essay in *The New York Review of Books*, titled "The Mystery of Consciousness," is illustrated with a "schematic drawing of a neuron, with its axon and dendrites reaching other neurons in a synaptic contact."[30] True to his materialist convictions, Searle offers this definition of consciousness:

The term "consciousness" refers to those states of sentience and awareness that typically begin when we awake from a dreamless sleep and continue until we go to sleep again, or fall into a coma or die or otherwise become 'unconscious.' . . . Consciousness so defined switches off and on. By this definition a system is either conscious or it isn't. . . . Consciousness is an ordinary biological phenomenon comparable with growth, digestion, or the secretion of bile. . . . The main task of a philosophy and science of consciousness right now is to show how consciousness is [biological] . . . along with digestion, photosynthesis, and all the rest of it.[31]

Emphasizing that "what in any case I want is a causal explanation of consciousness," Searle repeatedly asserts that the brain *causes* consciousness: "How exactly do neurobiological processes in the brain *cause* consciousness? . . . It is an amazing fact that everything in our conscious life . . . is *caused* by brain processes."[32] He also asserts that "Consciousness is caused by lower-level neuronal processes in the brain and *is itself a feature of the brain.*"[33] In other words, Searle makes consciousness (minding) an attribute of brains, not persons. Similarly, memories are not experiences that persons have; they are things that "we must *store* . . . somehow in the synaptic connections between neurons."[34]

In his highly lauded book, *The Rediscovery of the Mind*, Searle treats the mind and the brain as if they were the same thing, referring to "it" as the "mind/brain," as in the following sentence: "[Meaning] is grounded in the more biologically basic intrinsic intentionality of the mind/brain."[35] In ordinary speech, we attribute intention to a person. Searle attributes intention to the mind/brain, thus conforming to the academic tradition according to which a serious philosopher's writing must lack all relevance to real life. The following passage is typical:

[N]ature is profligate, and just as every male produces enough sperm to repopulate the earth, so we have a lot more neurons than we need for a hunter-gatherer existence. I believe that the phenomenon of surplus neurons—as distinct from, say, opposed thumbs—is the *key to under-standing* how we got out of hunter-gathering and produced philosophy, science, technology, *neuroses*, advertising, etc.[36]

Searle does not elaborate on bracketing neuroses with advertising, thus implying that they are not diseases. Instead, he discourses about "silicon brains" and "conscious robots," and concludes:

I see the human brain as an organ like any other, as a biological system. Its specific feature, as far as the mind is concerned . . . is its capacity to produce and sustain all of the enormous variety of our conscious life. . . . More than anything else, it is the neglect of consciousness that accounts for so much barrenness and sterility in psychology, the philosophy of mind, and cognitive science.[37]

Philosopher Karl Popper and neuroscientist John Eccles, coauthors of a treatise titled *The Self and Its Brain*, treat the brain as if it belongs to the self. Although libertarians often state that we have a right to self-ownership—which implies that the body and all its parts belong to the self or person—that is not at all what Popper and Eccles mean. What they mean is this: "[W]e regard the mind and its self-identity as crucial for personal identity; for, were we to think with Aristotle that the heart is the seat of the mind, we would expect personal identity to go with the heart rather than with the brain."[38]

Popper and Eccles try to explain the mind by equating it with "the personality," which they locate in the brain. They also conflate their personal experiences of self-identity with their minds and attribute the same "intellectualized" self-image to others. The result is epitomized by their weird speculations about brain transplants. They write:

And if we are asked why, in the case of a successful brain transplantation, we should expect the personality or the personal character to be transplanted . . . then we can hardly answer this question without speaking of the mind or the self; nor without speaking of its conjectural liaison with the brain . . . and we should have to predict (it would be a prediction testable in principle) that, after the transplantation, the person will claim identity with the donor of the brain and that he will be able to "prove" this identity. . . . we conjecture that due to this liaison the brain is the carrier of the self-identity of the person.[39]

I wonder what sorts of thought-experiments Popper and Eccles carried out to test their hypothesis? Their hypothesis implies that a person in Cleopatra's body possessing Marc Anthony's brain would believe that she/he is Marc Anthony; that a person in Romeo's body possessing Juliet's brain would believe that he/she is a woman. This is science? This is philosophy?

One of the most famous contemporary scientists writing about the mind is Francis Crick, Nobel Laureate and codiscoverer (with

James Watson) of the structure of DNA. In a book titled *The Astonishing Hypothesis* he argues that "'you,' your joys and your sorrows, your memories and your ambitions, your sense of personal identity and free will, are in fact no more than the behavior of a vast assembly of nerve cells and their associated molecules . . . each of us *is* the behaviors of a vast, interacting set of neurons."[40] If Crick thinks this is a new idea, it is because he is ignorant of the history of the mind and especially of the history of madness. Hippocrates (fourth century, B.C.) had already asserted that the mind is a function of the brain,[41] a facile equation that never lost its appeal. In 1819, as modern medicine was aborning, Sir William Lawrence (1783–1867), President of the Royal College of Surgeons, declared: "[T]he mind, the grand prerogative of man, [is] merely an expression of the function of the brain."[42]

Crick insists that his approach to the problem of the mind is "scientific," a claim he supports by denying agency to persons and attributing agency to things. In Crick's world, neural networks "learn";[43] and free will (capitalized) is an attribute of the cerebral cortex. He asks: "Where might Free Will be located in the brain?", and answers: "Free Will is located in or near the anterior cingulate sulcus."[44]

Lastly, one of the most influential recent contributors to the philosophy of the mind is Princeton psychologist Julian Jaynes. The text on the dust jacket of his best-selling *The Origin of Consciousness in the Breakdown of the Bicameral Mind* summarizes his thesis as follows:

Julian Jaynes shows us how ancient peoples . . . could not "think" as we do today, and were therefore "unconscious." Unable to think, they experienced auditory hallucinations—voices of gods, actually heard in the Old Testament or the *Iliad*—which, coming from the brain's right hemisphere, told the person what to do in circumstances of novelty or stress.[45]

Jaynes treats the mind as if it were the brain and attributes human progress to its evolution, especially to changes in the functional relations between the right and left cerebral hemispheres, hence his term, "bicameral mind." His basic assumption is that experiencing auditory hallucinations was the normal mental state of the ancient Greeks:

Iliadic man did not have subjectivity as we do; he had no awareness of his awareness of the world, no internal mind-space to introspect upon.

. . . Volition, planning, initiative is organized with no consciousness whatever and then "told" to the individual in his familiar language, sometimes with the visual aura of a familiar friend or authority figure or "god," or sometimes as a voice alone. The individual obeyed these hallucinated voices because he could not "see" what to do by himself. . . . we could say that before the second millennium B.C., *everyone* was schizophrenic."[46]

Asserting that 4,000 years ago everyone in Greece was schizophrenic may be sensational, but is nonsensical. We generally attach the diagnostic label "schizophrenic" to individuals who are economically (and usually also personally) dependent on others. Hence, everyone in a society cannot be schizophrenic, because there would be no one to take care of the "schizophrenics."

Jaynes's speculations about the Greeks' auditory hallucinations, unsupported and insupportable by evidence, express his own psychopolitical agenda and rest on his ignorance of the psychology and neurophysiology of "hearing voices." He writes: "Some people find it difficult to even imagine that there can be mental voices that are heard with the same experiential quality as externally produced voices. After all, there is no mouth or larynx in the brain! Whatever brain areas are utilized, it is absolutely certain that such voices do exist and that *experiencing them is just like hearing actual sound*."[47]

This is false. Neither experientially nor biologically is "hearing voices" like hearing another person speak. Eugen Bleuler, who first identified (invented) schizophrenia, himself noted that the person who claims to hear voices "hears" his own inner speech. This is confirmed by neuroimaging studies showing that, neurophysiologically, auditory hallucinations resemble speaking, not hearing.[48]

Dreams and hallucinations may be the only neuronic thoughts. Background static from synapses discharging.

Why, then, are these neurophilosophical speculations—that rest either on unproven fantasies or proven falsehood—important? One of the reasons they are is that the specialists who advance them, as well as the science writers who report them to the public, extol these ideas as good for us. Thus, Richard Restak, a neurologist and popular writer, compliments Crick for propounding the "*liberating notion* that each of us is, ultimately, the behavior of a vast and complex network of billions of neurons."[49] The claim that neurobiological reductionism is liberating is neither new nor true. Warren S. McCulloch—one of the undisputed fathers of modern neuroscience—was also interested in "scientific liberation." I had a chance to see McCulloch in action in Chicago in the late 1940s and early

1950s, when I was a young psychiatrist. I have not forgotten him. McCulloch wrote: "In Illinois a third of all State hospital inhabitants have senile psychoses. Pray for their speedy death or legislate for euthanasia, but waste no tears on them."[50] Doesn't anyone *listen* to the new scientists of the mind?

A MATHEMATICS OF MIND?

I shall now briefly consider some recent books on the mind written by mathematicians and mathematical physicists. Although scholars in these fields are usually not considered to be experts on psychology, and although their technical explanations are incomprehensible to the nonmathematician, their books occupy center stage in both the professional and popular literature on the mind.

One of the earliest works of this type is *Gödel, Escher, Bach* by Douglas Hofstadter, a cognitive and computer scientist at the University of Indiana.[51] The paperback edition is subtitled, "A Metaphorical Fugue on Minds and Machines in the Spirit of Lewis Carroll." Hofstadter's recent book, titled *Fluid Concepts and Creative Analogies*, is described as offering "a challenging new view of the mind . . . [by means of] computer models of the fundamental mechanisms of thought."[52] I can understand Lewis Carroll. But I cannot understand Gödel, Hofstadter, or Fluid Concepts and will therefore pass on.

The Mind as "Microtubule" and Other Fabulous Fantasies

Roger Penrose is Rouse Ball Professor of Mathematics at Oxford University. His first book on the foundations of human behavior, *The Emperor's New Mind*, received rave reviews and was on the *New York Times* best-seller list. His follow-up work, *Shadows of the Mind*, attracted even more critical attention.[53] In both works, Penrose combines ordinary English prose with mathematical notations whose meaning is unaccessible to anyone without a high level of competence in mathematics (assuming they make sense to mathematicians).

According to the text on the dust jacket, in *Shadows of the Mind* Penrose "contends that in consciousness some kind of global quantum state must take place across large areas of the brain, and that it is within microtubules [in the brain] that these collective quantum effects are most likely to reside." Despite the obvious similarity between locating the mind of the pineal gland and in microtubules, some reviewers were especially impressed by Penrose's thesis "that tiny constituents of our brain cells called microtubules could, by exploiting subtle quantum effects, act as the real engines of awareness and free will."[54]

To be able to follow Penrose's argument, the reader must be familiar with concepts and theories such as "Gödel's second incompleteness theorem," "Hilbert space descriptions," "Hilbert's tenth problem," "density matrices," "Diophantine equations," and "polynomial equations," to mention just a few.[55] I do not understand these concepts and theories and hence cannot comment on the use to which Penrose puts them. However, Hillary Putnam, a professor of philosophy at Harvard University, claims that Penrose's thesis is "a straightforward case of a mathematical fallacy."[56]

To an interviewer, Penrose explains that even the most sophisticated tools of current quantum physics are inadequate for the task of giving a mathematical, quantum-physical account of the mind: "We won't get the whole picture until we develop a new branch of physics . . . in consciousness we are actually using some physics that physicists don't know yet."[57] Here Penrose too replaces mind with consciousness and then "explains" the latter. John Searle also locates the crux of Penrose's thesis in this concept: "On the view that I [Searle quoting Penrose] am tentatively putting forward, consciousness would be some manifestation of this quantum-entangled internal cytoskeletal state and of its involvement in the interplay . . . between quantum and classical levels of activity."[58]

If less impressive authorities spoke like this, we might be inclined to smile, if not laugh. It is meaningless to give a psychological explanation to a mathematical concept, such as an imaginary number; we rightly call such efforts "psychobabble." I contend that it is just as meaningless to give a mathematical explanation to a psychological concept, such as consciousness; we should call such efforts "mathematicobabble." Notwithstanding the adulation lavished on Penrose's books, I dare say that their style exemplifies that jargon. Nevertheless, so great is Penrose's prestige that John Cornwell even praises his writings for being accessible to the general reader:

Penrose demonstrates that mathematics and physics are more central to the problems of consciousness than computer science or even biology. . . . his book may be the first accessible report to a general readership about the *site*, if not the actual substance, of the Holy Grail of consciousness—the precise point where quantum activity interacts with classical physical activity in the brain.[59]

Cornwell's judgment is flatly contradicted by physicist John Gribbin, who writes: "I could not recommend it [*Shadows of the Mind*] to anyone who doesn't have at least a degree in physics."[60] However, I recommend it to anyone who wants to see for himself Penrose's masterful masking of malarkey as the mathematics of the mind.

Penrose believes that explaining the mind mathematically supports the view that there is no God. Frank J. Tipler, a mathematical physicist at Tulane University, believes exactly the opposite, namely, that it proves the existence of God, resurrection, and all the assorted consolations of the Christian faith. Penrose and Tipler cannot both be right, though they could both be wrong.

The Physics of Immortality, Tipler's contribution to the mathematics of the mind, is an amazing inversion of the medieval Catholic doctrine that physics is a branch of theology.[61] He writes:

It is unique to find a book asserting, as I shall in the body of this book, that theology is a branch of physics, that physicists can infer by calculation the existence of God and the likelihood of the resurrection of the dead to eternal life in exactly the same way as physicists calculate the properties of the electron. . . . I have been forced into these conclusions by the inexorable logic of my own special branch of physics.[62]

Tipler's "inexorable logic" rests on redefining ordinary concepts and words, such as life, death, and person, as the following passage illustrates:

I therefore regard a human being as nothing but a particular type of machine, the human brain as nothing but an information processing device, the human soul as nothing but a program being run on a computer called brain. Further, all possible types of living beings, intelligent or not, are of the same nature, and subject to the same laws of physics as constrain all information processing devices.[63]

If "all possible types of living beings are of the same nature," then the chickens and carrots we have for dinner will also be resurrected. Tipler does not say this in so many words. He does, however, claim that the "loved pets of humans will be resurrected because their human owners want them to be."[64] Then, worried lest the reader think that Hitler might also be resurrected, he offers this piece of scientific explanation:

Said individual [a Hitler] may prefer to continue committing evil acts against other humans. The Omega Point will not permit this, for it would contradict the love which He/She bears for the simulated creatures. . . . Hell would exist because the Omega Point refuses to abandon a human no matter how evil; Hell's existence would be a testimony to the literally infinite love of the Omega Point for His/Her creatures.[65]

This passage resembles a pop-music icon's contorted explanation of the "real meaning" of his anti-Semitic lyrics more than a scientist's explanation of the workings of the human mind. Indeed, Tipler's confabulation quickly degenerates into a farcical facsimile of medieval angelology. Historians tell us that Saint Albert the Great calculated the exact number of angels in Heaven and found it to be 399,920,004.[66] Tipler has calculated the exact number of "human memories": "[T]he human brain can store between 10 to the 10th power and 10 to the 17th power bits . . . which implies that there are between 2 to the 10th power / to the 10th power and 2 to the 10th power / to the 17th power possible human memories."[67]

Paul Davies, a professor of natural philosophy at the University of Adelaide and a successful popularizer of physics, agrees with Tipler. He asserts that materialism is dead, that "there is no clear division . . . between what is living and what is not."[68] Appropriately, Davies was awarded the $1 million Templeton Prize for Progress in Religion in 1995 for his "numerous findings indicating that there is purpose and design to human existence."[69]

In his curiously self-centered book, *The Quark and the Jaguar*, famed mathematical physicist Murray Gell-Mann's approach to the problem of the "brain and mind" resembles Searle's. Gell-Mann takes it as self-evident that "the mind" and "consciousness" can be explained in terms of brain function. And, much like the other scientists whose writings I have reviewed, he also avoids addressing simple, everyday moral (mental) problems, such as how we determine which acts to praise and blame or how we decide whom to reward and punish. Instead, Gell-Mann prefers to offer science fiction speculations, such as the following: "Some day, for better or worse, such interconnections [between the neurons of two or more persons] might be possible. A human being could be wired directly to an advanced computer . . . and by means of that computer to one or more other human beings. Thoughts and feelings would be completely shared."[70] The prospect of such an interpersonal-neuronal hookup raises this question: Would synaptic-neuronal connections between a stupid and a smart person make them both equally stupid or equally smart?

"HORROR AND NEGLECT OF THE OBVIOUS"

As we have seen, Searle attributes "the barrenness and sterility in psychology, the philosophy of mind, and cognitive science" to a neglect of consciousness. Is this true? Or is this barrenness due to a neglect of real life, exemplified by his work and that of many other contemporary, materialist experts on the mind?

From a very different angle, C. S. Lewis had addressed and answered this question. In the *Screwtape Letters*, he casts the answer in the form of this advice Screwtape offers his pupil Wormwood: "Aggravate that most useful human characteristic, the horror and neglect of the obvious. You must bring him to a condition in which he can practice self-examination for an hour without discovering any of those facts about himself which are perfectly clear to anyone who has ever lived in the same house with him or worked in the same office."[71]

Although Isaiah Berlin was not addressing this specific question, his following warning is, in effect, a more elaborate answer to it:

[I]n the course of this [explaining human behavior in causal-deterministic terms] they [the materialists] describe the normal lives lived by men in terms which fail to mark the most important psychological and moral distinctions known to us. This they do in the name of an imaginary science; and, like the astrologers and soothsayers whom they have succeeded, cast up their eyes to the clouds, and speak in immense, unsubstantiated images and similes, in deeply misleading metaphors and allegories . . . Thereby they throw dust in their own eyes as well in ours, obstruct our vision of the real world, and further confuse an already sufficiently bewildered public.[72]

The Case Against Biological Reductionism

While many contemporary scientists support the claims of positivistic neuroscience, many others oppose them as grandiose pseudoscience and utopian (dystopian) political longing.[73] These critics caution that the very search for a relationship between brain and mind is epistemologically incoherent and hence futile. For example, Werner Heisenberg, one of this century's greatest physicists, stated:

We would never doubt that the brain acts as a physiological mechanism if treated as such; but for an understanding of psychic phenomena we would start from the fact that the human mind enters as object and subject into the scientific process of psychology. . . . one will nowadays be less inclined to assume that the concepts of physics, even those of quantum theory, can certainly be applied everywhere in biology or other sciences.[74]

For Michael Polanyi, accepting the limits of science is the beginning of scientific wisdom.[75] He wrote: "The recognition of certain basic impossibilities has laid the foundations of some major principles of physics and chemistry; similarly, recognition of the impossibility of understanding living things in terms of physics and chemistry, far from setting limits to our understanding of life, will guide it in the right direction."[76]

It is naive to believe that attributing mental functions to brain functions is a modern scientific discovery or that the dominant mechanical model of the age (now, the computer) is the right model for explaining the brain-mind. The writings of science popularizer John McCrone are illustrative. He declares: "The mind is like a combination of [computer] hardware and software—the hardware being the brain and the software being the habits of thought and mental skill that run upon it."[77] He also uses this analogy—which he calls the "bifold model"—to explain mental illness. Schizophrenia, he asserts, is "nothing more than . . . a crumbling of the fragile processes that produce the bifold mind. . . . Dreams and madness . . . [are] but the broken-backed functioning of the bifold mind."[78] This is tabloid science, not neuroscience.

Let us face the facts. The modern intellectual's search for the seat of the mind is but a new version of the medieval scholar's search for the seat of the soul. Descartes located the soul in the pineal gland. When science displaced religion, the mind replaced the soul and people began to look for the seat of the mind. Not surprisingly, they found it in the brain, rediscovering the "discovery" of the great pagan physician, Hippocrates, who stated: "Men ought to know that from nothing else but the brain come joy, despondency and lamentation. . . . By the same organ we become mad and delirious, and fears and terrors assail us."[79]

Mind and Brain: The Lesson of Language

Regardless of how dictionaries define the mind and how neuroscientists use the term, the words "mind" and "brain" are elements of everyday language that are often used interchangeably, as synonyms for one another. This is because we can use each of these terms literally as well as metaphorically. For example, we say "brainchild," for a creative idea; "brainless," for stupid; "brainstorm," for a sudden inspiration or a group meeting to solve a problem; "brainwashing," for coercive persuasion; "brainy," for intelligent; and "mind altering drug," for a chemical that affects the brain. Competent speakers of English understand that a brainless person is a stupid individual (metaphorically brainless), whereas a brainless cadaver is a dead body from which the pathologist has removed the brain (literally brainless).

Similarly, when a person says that he is "mad as hell," he does not mean that he feels sick. When he says, "I feel like giving him a piece of my mind," everyone (who knows English) understands that he does not feel like giving away a part of his brain. When a journalist wants to categorize a crime as particularly heinous, he calls it "mindless," not "brainless." The point is obvious. A brainless person cannot commit a crime, just as an eyeless person cannot see. Were a person to call an act "brainless," we would interpret it as a symptom of *his* inability to use English correctly, not as a symptom of the *actor's* alleged brain disease. *Ergo*, if mind is brain, and if the misbehaving person is not brainless, then he is not mindless. No further evidence or reasoning should be necessary to show that the mind is not the brain.*

The terms "brain" and "mind" belong to different conceptual categories and different modes of discourse. The brain is a bodily organ and a part of medical discourse. The mind is a personal attribute and a part of moral discourse. So long as we view personal conduct commonsensically, we attribute (bad) behavior to the mind or, more precisely, to the person who displays it. However, once we view such conduct psychiatrically (and legally), we typically attribute it to the brain: We say that the bad man is mad, or that the madman is bad, because he has a brain disease.[80] Thus, we often bracket the terms "violent" and "mental patient," but we never

---

*So long as we use the word "mind" as a synonym for the word "brain" (or as a noun that refers to some other medically relevant entity), we cannot seriously entertain the possibility that the term "mental illness" is an oxymoron.

bracket the terms "violent" and "brain patient." As I have argued earlier, the ideas of badness, madness, intention, and responsibility are so intertwined that this entire nexus must be considered intrinsic to the meaning of the term "mind."[81]

Consider, for example, a feature article in *Newsweek* illustrated with a cross section of the brain, captioned: "Mapping the Mind."[82] In an accompanying article, the reporter explains that in the future computers might "literally read your brain waves, your thoughts."[83] A cover story in *Time* magazine titled "Glimpses of the mind," is subtitled: "Science unravels the best-kept secrets of the human brain."[84] In all these examples, the terms "mind" and "brain" are used as we might use the terms "twelve" and "dozen." Richard L. Gregory, editor of the prestigious *Oxford Companion to the Mind*, also intermingles the two terms. He writes: "We all have a mind, but do we really know what it is, how the brain works?"[85] A professor of philosophy observes: "[P]eople have a considerable propensity to *identify* mind as brain. . . . in ordinary language such idioms as 'He has a good brain' and 'He has a good mind' are used almost interchangeably."[86]

Because scientific fashions are perhaps even more powerful than sartorial fashions, it is not easy to question the equation of mind and brain. Conventional wisdom mandates that we confuse brains with persons and accept certain psychiatric claims, such as the existence of "multiple personality" as a genuine brain disease. For example, David Oakley and Lesley Eames, two neuroscientists, flatly assert that "location of the self-representations underlying multiple personality . . . are cortical. . . . [A] split-brain operation . . . on a multiple personality case might be revealing."[87]

Like the word "mind," the word "personality" refers to an abstraction. John Doe is a person. He "has" no personality, except in the abstract sense in which he might also be said to "have" a sense of humor. Treating the "personality" as if it were like the spleen, and multiple personality as if it were like accessory spleens, is to confuse a social construct and a bodily organ. I maintain that attributing the mind to the brain is scientism, not science.

THE COVERT POLITICAL-ECONOMIC AGENDA OF NEUROSCIENCE

The present state of neuroscience reflects the results of a long-standing alliance between science and the state, specifically, between medicine (psychiatry) and the state. Since the 1950s, the

American people have been subjected to a relentless campaign of so-called mental health education, indoctrinating them into the belief that mental diseases are brain diseases, curable with chemicals.[88] Thus, the ostensible agenda of neuroscience is the quest for increased scientific understanding of the *brain*; its real agenda, however, is to elevate to the level of unquestioned "scientific fact" the doctrine that *(mis)behavior* is biologically determined and that holding individuals responsible for their *(mis)behavior* is unscientific. Michael Merzenich, a member of the Keck Center for Integrated Neuroscience at the University of California in San Francisco, puts it this way:

We operate on the principle that the laws of psychology that govern behavior are really brain laws that operate on a materialist philosophy. When Johnny can't read, there's an explanation in the brain. . . . when Billy has murderous intent, there is explanation for Billy's murderous intent. . . . Ultimately our plan constitutes a challenge to the societal assessments that led to the principles of common law [based on the presumption of free will].[89]

Note that Merzenich illustrates his thesis by reference to undesirable behaviors, such as a child's inability to learn to read. However, if brain laws explain behavior, they must also explain desirable behaviors, such as a child's ability to learn to read. Why do researchers avoid citing good behaviors as their examples? Because they realize that it would be absurd to try to explain the acquisition of complex skills, such as reading or writing or playing chess, without recourse to ordinary concepts, such as practice and self-discipline. Clearly, every physically able person can learn to articulate sounds and form letters; but it requires practice and self-discipline to become an orator or calligraphist. Similarly, every physically able person can act in the world, but it requires practice and self-discipline to become a responsible moral agent. By replacing moral discourse about bad behaviors with medical discourse about bad brains, it is precisely the concept of responsibility that neuroscientists and other reductionists want to destroy.[90]

In the future, Merzenich predicts, "the very principles of jurisprudence will come from an understanding of the principles of brain operation."[91] Philip E. Johnson, a professor of criminal law at the University of California in Berkeley, agrees: "If we could go to death row and show that the inhabitants have something wrong with their brains that could be fixed so they would become peaceful, productive members of society, obviously that would and should produce a tremendous change in the way we approach homicidal behavior."[92]

Such assertions imply that the brains of some persons lack certain chemicals necessary for moral agency. They must be given the chemicals they need, if necessary against their will, to enable them to act as moral agents. This gambit solves nothing. Suppose that after being so medicated, the subject still rejects being "helped." Would that be interpreted as evidence that he rightly rejects further treatment (which others want to impose on him)? Or as evidence that the treatment was ineffective (and that he requires further treatment)?

Brain-Mind Fantasy Meets the Real World

A space alien reading the works of experts who write about the mind as if it were the brain would have not the slightest inkling that the distinctions between these two categories affect the lives and occupy the day-to-day activities of legions of lawyers, judges, journalists, insurance company executives, psychiatrists, patients, and, in the end, every man, woman, and child in the country. The vignette below illustrates the reality that the neuroscientists and neurophilosophers systematically conceal or ignore.

Pat Roe (pseudonym), a woman described as a "highly compensated professional," is hospitalized with a diagnosis of bipolar disorder.* After leaving the hospital, she claims to be unable to work and begins to receive $11,000 *per month* from her insurer. Two years later, the insurance carrier notifies Roe that payments would terminate after twenty-four months, because her disability "was caused by 'mental illness,'" which the company defined as "any mental, nervous, or emotional diseases or disorders of any type."[93] No such limitation applied to disabilities caused by bodily illnesses. Roe sues. At the trial, psychiatrists testify "that substantial research evidence points to an organic basis and genetic transmission for bipolar disorder." One of the experts declares: "This disorder is just as organic as if your thyroid was cut off, and it was causing your metabolism in your body to be off." The judge rules

*Formerly called manic-depression.

that Roe is entitled to disability payments because bipolar illness is due to a brain disease and "a mental condition with an organic cause should be treated like any other illness."

The decision prompts the Aetna Life and Casualty Company, a large underwriter of health care policies, to issue this warning: "We have said a mental disorder is a disease commonly understood to be a mental disorder whether or not it has a physiological or organic basis and for which *treatment is generally provided by or under the direction of a mental health professional such as a psychiatrist, psychologist, or a psychiatric social worker.*"[94]

The consequences of the confusion between illness and the patient role—which characterizes our medical-psychiatric scene and to which I have called attention elsewhere—have come home to roost.[95] Mental illness is no longer defined as a disease a physician diagnoses or a patient has, but as "that" which a mental health professional "treats."[*]

If the mind were, in fact, the brain, there would be no justification for the existence of two separate medical specialties devoted to the diagnosis and treatment of diseases of the brain, neurology and psychiatry. If mental illnesses are brain diseases, they ought to be treated by neurologists and neurosurgeons—with the consent of the patient. The equation of brain and mind invalidates the legitimacy of the mental health professions and of involuntary psychiatric interventions. The following vignette in Alan J. Hobson's *The Chemistry of Conscious States* starkly illustrates these contradictions:

In this way [if we had known more about drugs earlier] we might have avoided the poignant dialogue that Bertal [one of Hobson's patients] and I had the day before he was to be transferred to that 1960s graveyard for the failed treatments, the Boston State Hospital. "I am sorry I was ever cured," Bertal said sadly, understanding somehow that we had raised his awareness of his problem but could offer him no solution. "You should have left me in the dream world."[96]

---

[*]According to this logic, if there were no mental health professionals, there would be no mental illnesses. *Mutatis mutandis*, if there were no doctors, there would be no diseases. Of course, this is nonsense. In the absence of medical or mental health professionals, there would still be diseases (bodily and "mental"); however, there would be no patients, because persons could not occupy the patient role (that is, have a formally defined social relationship with nonexistent professionals).

If Bertal was cured, why did Hobson send him to a "graveyard for the failed treatments"? If Bertal did not want to go that "graveyard," why did he go? Did he go involuntarily, because Hobson used his power as a psychiatrist to have him confined there? Hobson does not say.

"The Decade of the Brain": Neuroscience or Lyshenkoism?

The Congress of the United States of America has declared the 1990s to be "The Decade of the Brain." What does this mean? To Deborah Mash, chief of the University of Miami Medical School's Brain Endowment Bank, it means that "It wasn't just politics when Congress declared the nineties 'The Decade of the Brain.'"[97] It is a hollow protest. Whatever Congress does is, by definition, political. Dr. Carla Shatz, president of the Society for Neuroscience, proudly acknowledges that "Basic brain research is seeking answers that may ultimately help guide social policy."[98] I suggest that the slogan, "Decade of the Brain," is a code phrase to promote the belief that mental illnesses are brain diseases and to justify ever-increasing government funding for the war against these "diseases."

"The real proof that mental disorders are not different from other illnesses like cancer and heart disease," explains a health reporter in a typical feature article in the *Los Angeles Times*, "rests in brain imaging techniques that show how the brain is defective or sick. . . . Being able to actually see a sick brain . . . and then see it improve will help convince both the public and health insurers that many serious mental illnesses are biologically based."[99] At the same time, down the street from offices of the *Los Angeles Times*, the Neuropsychiatric Institute of UCLA is advertising for volunteers in a study of the chemical treatment of "major depression" in adolescents. The flyer offers free treatment and compensation "up to $350" for qualifying subjects. What are the requirements for qualification? "Subjects will be eligible if they are between the ages of twelve years zero months and eighteen years and eleven months, have exhibited symptoms of depression for at least eight weeks, and are in *good physical health*."[100] Having sick brains is evidently compatible with being in good physical health.

The claim that "major" mental illnesses are brain diseases can no longer be questioned. It is a fact. Hence, doctors need to study brains. Marian Diamond, a neuroscientist at the University of

California at Berkeley, explains: "Donated brain tissue is crucial to studies of an astonishing range of afflictions. . . . by the year 2000, we hope to have a better grasp . . . about diseases like schizophrenia . . . [and] depression."[101]

Where do the donated brains go? To so-called brain banks, of which there are several in the country. One is at the McLean Hospital in Cambridge, Massachusetts, a psychiatric facility affiliated with Harvard Medical School. Its director, Dr. Edward Bird, states: "Mental illnesses are real diseases like cancer or arthritis, but we have to educate them [the public]."[102] To accomplish that goal, the bank distributes a bumper sticker that reads: "RESEARCH TAKES BRAINS, 1-800-BRAIN-BANK." Dr. Bird also evangelizes through the National Alliance of the Mentally Ill (NAMI), whose newsletter advertises the brain bank at McLean and exhorts: "Schizophrenia is a brain disease."[103]

It appears that the vast majority of Americans have abandoned the distinction not only between mental illnesses and brain diseases but also between the mind and the brain, or hold the view that the mind is secreted by the brain much as urine is secreted by the kidney. For example, Itiel Dorr, a professor of psychology at Miami University in Ohio, asserts that "The brain is an information-processing device. It can be expanded to increase processing capacity or memory just like you may add RAM or upgrade your CPU on a personal computer"; and he speculates about "extending your brain-processing ability by adding microchips [to the brain] . . . enhancing specific abilities such as a mathematical co-processor, or implanting ready-made knowledge."[104]

In a similar vein, Scott Grader, a Manhattan attorney, mistakes thoughts for things and predicts "A machine that would take thought-processes and put them directly onto a computer. Forget about writing or dictating. You simply think your thoughts and they go directly into your computer." Perhaps because lawyers love to use the literalized metaphor of mental illness in their pleadings, they are especially gullible consumers of neuroscientistic foolishness. Thus, Joan Gmora, also a New York attorney, wonders about "a machine that would read a book for you. You would still absorb all the information, but it would go directly into your brain. You'd get the enjoyment and the education, but it would be instantaneous and save you a lot of time. . . . I'd like to see a replacement for sleep. . . . Think of the time you'd save." Apparently lawyers do not dream of a machine that would copulate and have an orgasm "for you" and thus "save you a lot of time."* Note the disappearance, in these futuristic dreams, of persons who speak, learn, have experiences, and are responsible for their behavior.

Finally, a comment in the letters column of the *New York Times Magazine* illustrates the intellectual irresponsibility that regularly attends the arguments that rest on equating mind with brain. A reader writes: "The traditional but nonetheless specious distinction between mind and brain has spawned an equally false dichotomy between psychotherapy and psychiatric medications. . . . once inside the brain, words and medications are substantively equivalent."[105] If the assertion that "inside the brain, words and medications are substantively equivalent" means anything (other than fashionable hype), it means either that we would have to treat words as we treat drugs and repeal the First Amendment, or that we would have to treat drugs as we treat words and repeal the drug laws. I believe most Americans would strongly oppose both of these measures. So much for taking language seriously.

No amount of incoherence and self-contradiction seems to deter the faithful. They tirelessly proclaim the Truth, as revealed to them by Neuroscience. Bill Moyers, a leading evangelist, pontificates: "When the regulation of chi, or vital energy, is the object of medicine, questions about mind and body make no sense."[106] Richard Restak, who should know better, declares: "The traditional distinction between mind and brain embodied in the two often-competing disciplines of psychiatry and neurology is now untenable."[107] This statement rests on the false premise that psychiatrists deal with brains (or minds), when in fact they deal with persons (in conflict with others and/or themselves). Actually, psychiatrists and neurologists do not compete for the same territory: The former deal with persons who misbehave or are unhappy; the latter, with persons whose brains "misbehave" or who suffer from the effects of neurological diseases.

Of course, psychiatrists and neurologists have long maintained that psychiatry and neurology are "the same." Far from being based on new scientific discoveries, this claim represents a return to the neuropsychiatry of the nineteenth century, that is, the period before neurology and psychiatry became separate disciplines. Taking this

---

*I cite this material to illustrate the sorts of ideas about the mind the *New York Times* takes seriously enough to print in its Business Section, under the caption of "Patents."

claim seriously would require that medical schools merge the two departments and abolish either neurology or psychiatry. I know of no neurologist or psychiatrist who supports such a policy.

Hypocrisy, remarked La Rochefoucauld, is the homage vice pays to virtue.

5

Mind: The History of an Idea

I have tried to show that although the word "mind," like the words "beauty" or "love," names something real and important, "it" does not exist in space and cannot be located in, or attributed to, an organ. Although this view is far from novel,[1] its full scope and implications have remained undeveloped. As a result—and because we live in an age blessed by the fruits of materialist science—reductionist ideas about the relationship between mind and brain, such as I have reviewed, are more popular than ever.

What is the mind? The *Encyclopedia of Philosophy* states: "The fact of the matter is that there does not as yet exist a very satisfactory account of our concept of the mind."[2] Since there is no mind, this is not surprising. It is also not surprising that, nevertheless, philosophers and scientists have given us, and continue to give us, many answers to the question posed above. From René Descartes (1596–1650) until the nineteenth century, the mind was considered to be the secular successor to the soul, the attribute that distinguishes man from other living beings. Sigmund Freud (1856–1939) called the mind the "mental apparatus" and viewed it as a manifestation of the activity of the brain. Modern philosophers and neuroscientists assert that the mind is the brain, while mathematicians and physicists offer quantum-mechanical explanations not only of the mind but of God as well. I am trying to clarify this muddle by taking seriously that "mind" is a verb not an entity, and that we must seek the meaning of a word in its practical uses.

ANCIENT GREECE AND MODERN AMERICA

In Homer's time (ninth century, B.C.), the Greek language had no word for the mind or, strange as it may seem, for the living body. Until the fifth century, B.C., the word *soma*, rendered into English as body, denoted only the dead body or corpse.* "We find it difficult," warned Bruno Snell, author of the classic *Discovery of the Mind*, "to conceive of a mentality which made no provision for the body as such."[3]

The Greek term *psyche*—that forms the root of many English words—meant neither soul nor mind. Instead, it referred to a life force—a noncorporeal, immortal spirit—that left the body at the moment of death and migrated to Hades. The verb *psychein* means "to breathe," presaging the biblical legend of creation that identifies God's breath as the ensouling life force. It is unclear what the function of the *psyche* was during man's lifetime. The classic Greek term closest to mind was not *psyche*, but *menos*, which meant both spirit and intent. The latter meaning of *menos* is displayed in words such as *mimneskein*, to remind, and *mimeisthai*, to imitate or represent, whose root forms the English word *mime*.

Since language refracts reality, much as a lens refracts the image we see, the Greeks must have seen the world very differently from the way we see it. The Greek world was divided into two basic classes, *physis* and *nomos* (nature and convention), the former exemplified by the capacity for speech, the latter by the rules of a particular language. Our world is divided into matter and spirit, science and religion, fact and value, brain and mind, event or happening and behavior or action.

Our respective ideas of the "good life" are also different. For the Greeks of antiquity, the lives of human beings were a kind of shadow-play of the lives of the gods. The more closely a person's life resembled the heroic lives of gods, the more admirable and desirable it was. "Those closest to God," wrote Snell, "are not the poor and the meek, but the strong and the powerful."[4] Correlatively, those farthest from God are the cowardly and timid, whose behavior, deficient in will power, the Greeks viewed as foolish or deluded. Thus, it was the righteous man who heard the voices of the gods,

---

*English has only one word for the living body, but German has two: *Körper*, from the Latin *corpus*, denotes primarily the physical body; and *Leib*, cognate with English "life," refers specifically to the living human body. The dead body is called *Leiche*.

who counseled him to lead a life of courage-as-virtue. In contrast, today it is the insane person who hears God's voice, who counsels him to engage in mayhem-as-mental-illness.

The Politics of Virtue

Virtue is moral excellence. The meaning we give to this word thus depends on, and reflects, our idea of right living. It is instructive to examine the differences between the Aristotelian idea of right living and our idea of it.

We are familiar with the term *polis* in its English derivation, as in politics. However, we are unfamiliar with its Greek meaning, for which there is no equivalent English word. The best way to understand the Greek sense of *man in polis* is by reference to its opposite, man as natural slave. We believe that man is endowed by a Creator with inalienable rights and view freedom and slavery as *political* conditions. The Greeks entertained no such belief and viewed human beings as *naturally* divisible into persons who could govern themselves and those who could not.[5] We regard liberty as a morally neutral condition, which the person may put to virtuous or wicked use, and of which he may be deprived, "justly" or "unjustly," with or without "due process." The Greeks regarded liberty as synonymous with virtue, a condition the person could forfeit, by insufficient self-control or intemperance. This view—which is not wholly foreign to us—meshed with their belief that only certain persons could be self-governing, able to form and be members of the *polis* (that is, certain Greek-speaking, male adults); all others were regarded as unable to govern themselves and therefore unfit to be a part of the political community.

This conception formed the basis of Aristotle's political philosophy and of Plato's *Republic*, which is a blueprint of a caste society in which each person plays the role for which he is best "fitted." Henry Jaffa's summary of Aristotle's conception of the natural slave is helpful in this connection:

That there are natural slaves, in the aforesaid sense, is the universal experience of mankind. Today we call them mental incompetents . . . Aristotle is emphatic that those who are called slaves, but who are in fact competent, are not slaves by nature, but by law and convention only, and that the slavery of such men does rest, at bottom, upon force. There is a common interest which unites the natural slave with the natural master, but this is not true when unjust law and force alone are the ground of the relationship. Who is truly a master, and who is truly a slave, depends upon the *intrinsic characteristics of master and slave*.[6]

In short, the Greeks excluded nonresponsible persons—infants and others unable to control themselves—from membership in the *polis*. We include many persons unable to control themselves—exemplified by the insane—as members of the political community. Indeed, we insist on according them the right to vote and thus the opportunity to control those members of the community who are able to control themselves and who support those who are unable to do so.

Since the Greeks viewed the capacity for self-control as a personal virtue based on a gift of nature, it would have made no sense for them to hold a freeman who claimed to "hear voices" not responsible for his misdeeds, much less to coerce him to live rightly. In contrast, we use the concept of mind as if it were the "organ of excuses" and attribute a deficiency of culpability to "it" (caused by the abuses "it" endured in the past or the illnesses that afflict "it" at present). This is why we regard the impulse to reform the undisciplined adult as a virtue and accept that coercing him to lead a healthier life is adequate justification for using the power of the state to deprive him of liberty (and "treat" him against his will for [mis]behaviors we call "diseases"). It seems to me that if Aristotle had used the concept of mind, he would have identified it as the "organ of responsibility," would have attributed the faculty of accountability to "it," and would have claimed that only members of the *polis* possessed "it."

In the Greek philosophy of life, the principles of right living are epitomized by *sophronein* and *sophrosein*, that is, self-control and moderation. In the contemporary American philosophy of life, the principles of right living are epitomized by diagnosis and treatment solemnized by submission to medical-statist authority.* We have, in effect, inverted the Greek ideal of right living, treating self-control as an illusion and intemperance as an illness. Having equated virtue with health, we are left with only negative criteria for right

---

*The virtuous (sane) person submits to diagnosis and treatment voluntarily, because he recognizes that he is ill. The wicked person is compelled to submit to them by force, because he denies that he is ill and because medical interventions serve his own best interest.

living. Hence, we view bodily health as the absence of physical disease, mental health as the absence of mental disease, and prefer foolish chatter about healthy life styles to serious thought about articulating an authentic answer to the challenge of living a good life and choosing a good death. The phrase, "healthy life style," is itself a mask for concealing phobic maneuvers aimed at avoiding the dangers of life, both real and imaginary—especially the temptations of drugs and sex. Like Santayana's fanatic who redoubles his effort after he forgets his goal, we forget that health is a means not an end, and redouble our effort to become healthy. To aid and abet this folly, we create a corps of medical ethicists and invest them with a pseudoscientific professional role that effectively inhibits them from thinking seriously about life and death. Bereft of criteria for "right minding," our struggle for more and better "health care" drives us ever deeper into economic ruin and spiritual blindness.

Gilbert Ryle, let us recall, criticized the mind-matter dualists for postulating a "ghost in the machine."[7] It was a cogent counterweight against the traditional dualist-materialist argument, but it failed to take into account that, in everyday English, the word "mind" functions not only as if it were an agent or cause, but also as if it were an agency to which it is proper to attribute intentionality and nonintentionality, guilt and innocence.[8] This is precisely one of the aspects of mind that advocates of mathematical-physical approaches to the mind ignore. I am saying here that the term "mind" (in large part) belongs to the same family of words as, say, "contract" and "crime" belong; and that it is a fundamental mistake to treat the term "mind" as if its referent were a biological concept or entity, that is, as if it belongs to the same family of words as, say, "brain" and "blind." This error makes the effort to use mathematical and physical concepts to explain the mind just as absurd as would be the effort to use such concepts to explain crime and punishment.

A BRIEF HISTORY OF THE MIND

The modern concept of mind as a noncorporeal entity—separate from the body and yet in reciprocal communication with it—is supposed to originate with the great French philosopher, Descartes. Although this view is widely accepted, it is false, the product of mistranslation.

René Descartes: From Soul to Mind

Descartes' first substantial work, written in Latin, was the uncompleted treatise *Regulae ad Directionem Ingenii* (1628). The English philosopher Bernard Williams renders this as *Rules for the Direction of the Mind*.[9] This translation may be serviceable, but it is not quite right. The Latin word *ingenium* has a very different cognitive texture from the Latin word *mens*. Traupman's *New College Latin & English Dictionary* translates *ingenium* as "innate or natural quality, nature, temperament, character, bent, inclination, natural ability, talent, genius, clever person."[10] In contrast, the Latin *mens* meant not only mind, but also soul, reason, thought, and intention.

Descartes' choice of the word *ingenium,* suggests that he was referring not to rules governing the behavior of the mind, but to rules for developing each person's "innate direction" toward the morally good life. My contention that Descartes was not talking about what we call the mind is supported by the fact that when he wrote in French he always used the word *l'âme.** His last work, written in 1645, was titled *Les passions de l'âme*, which appears in a definitive English translation as *The Passions of the Soul*.[11] That is exactly right. In that sentence, French and English correspond word for word. To repeat, neither the Latin *ingenium*, nor the French *âme* means mind. It is puzzling, therefore, how the mind-body dichotomy came to be attributed to Descartes. It seems probable that all Descartes wanted to do was to impart scientific credibility to the theological concept of soul.

I read *The Passions of the Soul* and must admit that—except for a few passages, some of which I quote below—I found it incomprehensible. The gist of Descartes' thesis—that the soul is incorporeal but is located in the pineal gland—is simply self-contradictory. Under a heading, "What the functions of the soul are," he wrote: "After having thus considered all the functions which pertain to the body alone, it is easy to recognize that there is nothing in us which we ought to attribute to our soul excepting our thoughts."[12] By assigning thoughts to the soul, Descartes implicitly attributed consciousness and intentionality to it, features that enabled man, alone in the animal kingdom, to use language and possess free will.

---

*As I noted earlier, there is no French noun corresponding to the English "mind."

How did Descartes get the soul into the body? By assigning to it the function of thinking. He wrote:

The soul exercises its functions . . . [in] the brain . . . But in examining the matter with care, it seems as though I had clearly ascertained that the part of the body in which the soul exercises its functions immediately is . . . [not] the whole of the brain, but merely the most inward of all its parts, to wit, a certain very small gland which is situated in the middle of its substance. . . . Let us then conceive here that the soul has its principal seat in the little gland which exists in the middle of the brain.[13]

Why did Descartes select the pineal gland as the seat of the soul? Because it is a single—that is, not bilateral—organ which, he mistakenly believed, does not occur in any other animal. This claim imparted seemingly scientific support for the religious belief that animals have no souls. Although when the body dies, the pineal gland perishes along with it, and although Descartes referred to the soul as a "substance . . . closely joined to the brain," he nevertheless maintained that the soul is "immortal" and survives the death of the body.[14]

Descartes supported his claim that the seat of the soul is the pineal gland by appealing to his expertise in anatomy. Similarly, neuroscientists and psychiatrists support their claim that the seat of the mind is the brain by appealing to their expertise in neuro-chemistry and neuroimaging. If I interpret Descartes' thesis correctly, it is a mistake to blame him for the division of the human being into body and mind and to name this dichotomy "Cartesian." Instead, it would be more accurate to view him as a pioneer neuromythologist, the first to claim to have discovered evidence for locating the soul inside the cranium.

Despite this historical record, Descartes is viewed as the Columbus of the mind. Actually, Descartes maintained only that the body is matter, whereas the soul/mind is thought. One of his favorite sayings was: *L'âme pense toujours* (the soul thinks always). Presumably, what he meant is that "soul" and "thought" were two words for the same thing, much as neuroscientists now assert that "mind" and "brain" are two words for the same thing. In this light, the maxim, *Cogito ergo sum* (I think therefore I am), that made Descartes famous, is simply a reassertion of his faith in having a soul and his belief that possessing that precious gift is manifested by our ability to think. This interpretation is supported by his view that "the thing that thinks" survives the death of the body, because it is immaterial and imperishable. Bernard Williams aptly characterized Descartes' system as "a religious and dualistic metaphysics."[15]

Deus Ex Machina, Mens Insana Ex Medicina

The notion that God and Mind are the same thing is a thread that runs through much of Western thought. Menander, a fourth century, B.C., playwright, regarded *psyche* as identical with God.[16] The biblical Jews believed that God and the Word are the same thing.[17] According to Islamic scholars, "God first created the Pen. He said, Write."[18] Benedict Spinoza (1632–1677) asserted that "the mind and the body are one and the same thing"; that man is a "single system which has two names, 'God' and 'Nature;'"[19] and that "God is the free cause of all things."[20] Mary Baker Eddy (1821–1910), the founder of Christian Science, declared: "God is Mind."[21] Physicist Frank J. Tipler claims: "[P]hysicists can infer by calculation the existence of God."[22]

What is going on here? The answer is Colin Turbayne's remark that "We tend to forget that there are many subjects that we speak of only in metaphor . . . for example, the mind and God."[23] In this case, moreover, our Master Metaphor—combining the ancient idea of soul, the modern idea of mind, and the perennial idea of God—serves the purpose of masking the mystical concept of an *all-explanatory cause* as science.

An earlier, religious form of this concept is contained in the philosophy of the Talmud. Jewish mystical tradition holds that God's activity is not limited to a one-time Creation. According to the English-Jewish scholar Isidore Epstein, God's unceasing activity is required to "preserve the world He called into existence from collapsing into non-being. Were God to withdraw His providence but for a single moment, the whole existence would collapse into nothingness. This is the truth which Scripture never tires of asserting."[24] In short, *God is the Mind that never stops minding its business, which is Everything: He is intentionality incarnate.* *

---

*Controlling people as well as objects with the Word is the epitome of word magic. In short, the psychiatric idea of Mental Disorder as unintelligibility and nonintentionality is the mirror image of the religious idea of God as Order and Cause.

The sociologist Morse Peckham has convincingly demonstrated the unity of the ideas of God and mind as Ultimate Causes. He observed that "The something that the word [mind] allegedly names does not exist," and concluded that it is a notion whose function is to explain both the predictability and the unpredictability of human behavior.[25] Our need for explanations has a quasi-biological urgency, similar to our need for air or food. Hence, "social interaction without explanation is inconceivable: it may be the very condition of human existence."[26] Because we find questions without answers intolerable, we constantly manufacture explanations, most of which are inaccurate or incoherent. That does not matter. Inexplicability must be satisfied and "everybody is satisfied by *any* explanation some of the time."[27] Peckham concluded that the ideas of God and mind are (nothing but) explanatory strategies:

They [inexplicable phenomena] must be caused and caused, moreover, by unobservable (not, note, unobserved) forces. The unobservable force-producing entity for which a word exists is the mind. Therefore, if the responder judges himself to be culturally modern, he asserts that such phenomena are mentally produced. If he is willing to be judged more old-fashioned . . . he uses another word which is said to refer to an unobservable force-producing entity, God.[28]

The validity of this formulation is supported by the fact that virtually all modern intellectuals—from popularizers of pseudo-science such as Bill Moyers, to serious thinkers such as Aldous Huxley, to respected scientists such as Cornell University cosmologist Carl Sagan—believe that the mind can be the "cause" of both illness and health. Huxley scoffed at the idea of God as a cause, but believed that "Mind not only makes sick, it also cures."[29] Sagan asserted that "The mind can *cause* certain diseases."[30] Because we reify the mind and view it as an entity, the fallacy of attributing causal agency to "it" is deeply ingrained in our thinking.

To gain a better understanding of the fallacy intrinsic to the idea of mind-as-cause, we might consider the similarity between it and the familiar literary device called *deus ex machina* (God out of a machine), which refers to the author's introducing an unexpected and improbable occurrence to rescue his hero or heroine from a seemingly hopeless situation; for example, a poor widow with young children who is about to be evicted from her home suddenly inherits a large sum from an unknown relative. The expression is said to "have its origin in ancient Greek theater, especially in certain plays of Euripides. When the complexities of plot and character appeared incapable of resolution, a god was sent down on stage by mechanical crane to sort things out and make them right. Greek gods could do anything."[31]

Today, the mind can do anything. If it does something exceptionally admirable, we say that the agent who does it has the "mind of a genius." If it does something exceptionally repugnant, we say that the agent who does it has the "mind of a madman." In short, just as playwrights and novelists use the device called *deus ex machina,* so neuroscientists use the device we might call *mens ex machina,* and psychiatrists use the device *mens insana ex medicina*. Psychiatrists claim, and most people now believe, that mental illness *causes* addiction, crime, suicide, and countless other acts we abhor or fear. Therein lies the virtually limitless power of mental illness and psychiatry to undermine the idea of responsibility and subvert justice.

Despite intense scientific interest in the mind, the analogy between soul and mind has not lost its force. For most people, the soul is a quasi-explanatory construct to satisfy their speculation about life in the hereafter; similarly, the mind is a quasi-explanatory construct to satisfy their speculation about life here on earth. In medieval paintings, the soul is depicted as the spirit that leaves the dying body through the mouth and flies up to heaven or is cast down into hell; in modern illustrations, the mind is depicted as a part of the brain whose function is to account for what philosophers call "privileged access" (to the contents of our minds), and psychologists call "introspection" (into our inner life). In addition, the term "mind" is often used in lieu of the term "person," as in William Sargant's tale of brainwashing, titled *The Battle for the Mind*.[32]

The idea that introspected ideas or emotions are secrets—securely hidden from others but available to us by in(tro)spection of our own minds—confuses rather than clarifies the nature of mind. As an example of "privileged access to one's mental events," the author of the entry for the mind-body problem in the *Encyclopedia of Philosophy* cites "thoughts that cause the heart to pound . . . and feelings that cause a person to tremble."[33] This is an astonishingly naive statement, missing the point that, say, fear *is* a thought-and-feeling that we experience cognitively (mentally) as a thought, and physiologically (bodily) as trembling. The writer of the entry concludes: "The mind-body problem remains a source of acute discomfort to philosophers. . . . It may well be that the relation between mind and body is an ultimate, unique, and unanalyzable one."[34] This is true only if we persist in treating the word "mind" as a noun.

Consciousness and Intentionality Reconsidered

The words "mind" and "mental" can be used to denote either a set of capacities such as attending or intending, or a state of consciousness such as being awake and alert. Although in this book I have focused mainly on mind as attending and intending, since the term is often used to refer to consciousness—and then dealt with as if our problem were to explain "it"[35]—I want to say a few words about this concept.

As a rule, we use the word "consciousness" as a synonym for being awake and responsive to the environment, in contrast to being asleep and (more or less) unresponsive to it. Blows on the head and sedative drugs can render a person unconscious; alarm clocks and good books can make him conscious. Insofar as we equate mind with consciousness, the Freudian concept of unconscious mind is a metaphor squared as well as an oxymoron: The former, because the mind alone is a metaphor;* the latter, because the mind is conventionally defined as consciousness.

To be sure, the term "unconscious mind" may be a picturesque and useful name for an imaginary—deeply buried, cave-like—location where we hide our ideas that we do not want to acknowledge or want to forget or have in fact forgotten.[36] However, Freud's dual claims—that he "discovered the unconscious mind" and that psychoanalysis is "the science of the unconscious mind"—must be seen as the grandiose tactics of self-promotion that they are. An antibiotic, like penicillin, is discovered and can be studied scientifically. A fictitious mental location, like the unconscious mind, is invented and cannot be studied scientifically. This is not to gainsay Freud's contributions to our understanding of human behavior, for example, his rediscovery of the ancient insight that during sleep the brain remains active and continues to mind. The value of his work, however, is more than cancelled by the fact that the concept of

---

*The language of psychoanalysis is replete with self-contradictory metaphors, for example, unconscious intention.

unconscious mind is an invitation to virtually unlimited moral mischief: It lets anyone—especially persons accredited as experts on the mind—attribute any idea or motive to the unconscious mind of the Other and, at the same time, prevents the Other from convincingly invalidating and repudiating the attribution.[37]

Popper

Rationalist philosophers, unlike psychoanalysts, rightly emphasize the identity of mind with consciousness, and of consciousness with intentionality. The following statement by C. H. Whiteley is illustrative: "Anything is credited with a mind if it can act in ways which are likely to achieve some goal or other. . . . It is in this sense that we talk of mental deficiency."[38] In this sense, higher animals and even machines may be said to have minds; but this image obscures the differences between human (literal) mindings and nonhuman (metaphorical) mindings. The criminal who shoots the bank guard "has" intentionality, that is, chooses to rob, to carry a gun, and so forth; in contrast, the phototropic plant does not choose to seek sunlight and the heat-seeking missile "has" no intentionality (its intentionality being a creation of the men who build, aim, and fire it). Human minding entails knowledge of one's own heeding, in a word, self-conversation.

Although Whiteley ignores the dreamer's capacity to mind, he offers useful observations about the connections between consciousness and intentionality. "We commonly take for granted," he writes, "that there are many things which a wide-awake man (or dog or crocodile) can do, but a sleeping or comatose man (or dog or crocodile) cannot do; and furthermore that the wide-awake man can only do them . . . if he gives his mind to them, that is, keeps on being aware of them. The list of these capacities is very long."[39] Among the capacities that require intention, Whiteley lists writing poetry, planning, advertising, and swimming. In contrast, reflex actions, such as breathing and digesting, "can be elicited even from sleeping men."[40]

Lastly, I want to mention the views of the American sociologist-philosopher, George Herbert Mead, whose writings have greatly influenced my thinking. Mead was the first person to clearly state that the mind—as we use this term today—refers to a novel historical phenomenon, namely, the relationship between modern society and the independent, responsible individual.[41] He also emphasized that mind is mediated through language and that "the distinguishing trait of selfhood resides in the capacity of the minded organism to be an object to itself."[42] In short, language enables us to distinguish between the "I" and the "me" and to engage in self-conversation.

Mead consistently resisted identifying the mind as either noun or verb. Instead, he opted for a purely abstract conception of it, identifying mind with a particular attitude of the self, which he formulated as follows: "To the extent that the animal can take the attitude of the other and utilize that attitude for the control of his own conduct, we have what is termed mind; and that is the only apparatus involved in the appearance of mind."[43] Mead's resolute association of mind with self-reflection, self-control, and responsibility is only a short step from identifying the mind as the dialogue within. Thus, anticipating Bakhtin, Mead wrote: "If individuals are so distinguished from each other that they cannot identify themselves with each other, if there is not a common basis, then there cannot be a whole self present on either side."[44]

This is an important but incomplete formulation. We must not forget that an individual's nonidentification with the Other may be a matter of unwillingness rather than inability; or that in relationships that are *a priori* nonreciprocal—such as between child and adult, or patient and psychiatrist—we automatically attribute half a mind to the dominated, and a mind-and-a-half to the dominator.*

---

*I borrow this witticism from Karl Kraus, who defined an aphorism as a half-truth or a truth-and-a-half.

6

Modernity's Master Metaphors: Mental Illness and Mental Treatment

This book is about the mind, not the illnesses that allegedly afflict it or the treatments that allegedly restore its health. It is not a coincidence, however, that my present effort to analyze the mind as minding is of a piece with my past efforts to analyze mental illnesses as disapproved communications, and mental treatments as rhetoric, religion, or repression, disguised as "therapy."[1]

In this concluding chapter, I want to briefly reconsider mental illness (wrong-minding) and mental treatment (the attempt to restore right-minding) as the master metaphors of our age.

CRAZY TALK

Although touch, vision, and smell are important modalities of human communication, speaking and hearing are the most compelling. The primacy of speaking and hearing may account for the fact that desocialized, lonely persons talk crazy and hear crazy much more often than they see crazy. The belief that these behaviors are the symptoms of serious mental diseases, typically schizophrenia, is an integral part of psychiatric doctrine.[2]

From Language to Lesion

The publication of Rudolf Virchow's *Cellular Pathology* in 1858 signaled the birth of medicine as a profession based on modern science. However, no sooner was cellular pathology established as the objective (materialist) criterion of illness than it began to be expanded by the claim that the "senseless" speech of mental patients—a subjective (nonmaterialist) criterion—was a manifestation of disordered thinking which, in turn, was indicative of cellular pathology in the speaker's brain. Bleuler's invention of schizophrenia in 1911 completed the psychiatric transformation of language from a distinctively human characteristic into a "biological" marker of brain disease.

The neural connections could have been distorted by Will, and therefore appear to be a cause rather than an effect

For many years, psychiatrists only suspected that insanity was a genuine illness. Today, they insist that they know it is. Yet, this belief continues to rest on shaky grounds. For example, in a review of "the puzzle of schizophrenia," Julius Leff, a prominent British psychiatrist, acknowledges that "there is no pathological test for schizophrenia," and then declares: "Nevertheless, there are still enough casualties of the system for anyone to form an opinion as to whether schizophrenia is a myth or a diagnostic entity by holding a conversation with their local bag lady or man."[3] Leff's conclusion rests on confusing diagnoses with diseases, and on treating conversation as a valid method of ascertaining whether a person suffers from a brain disease.[4]

Frustrated by my argument that schizophrenia fails to meet the Virchowian criterion of disease, Sir Martin Roth, professor of psychiatry at the University of Cambridge, acknowledges: "Of course, if illness is a matter of lumps, lesions and germs, most schizophrenics are perfectly healthy."[5] Indeed so. This is why psychiatrists define pathological speech as a diagnostic marker of disease. However, no amount of research can bridge the gap between tissue and talk, between abnormal cells and abnormal speech, between pathology and psychopathology.

For obvious reasons, psychiatrists prefer to say that schizophrenics suffer from a "thought disorder" to saying that they, the psychiatrists, cannot understand their communications. I refrain from using the psychiatric locution because it implies that the observer knows how or what the subject thinks (when in fact he knows only what the subject says and what the listener hears or understands), and because it prejudges the observer as a normal expert and the subject as an abnormal patient.

Translating Bleuler: *"Sprachfehler"* is not "thought disorder"

Since it was Bleuler who coined the term "schizophrenia" and defined "it" as a disease, I believe we ought to take note of the differences between what he wrote and what those who rely solely on the English translation of his work believe that he wrote.

Although English and American psychiatrists routinely state that "thought disorder" is one of the cardinal characteristics of schizophrenia,[6] this term does not appear in anything resembling its German equivalent in Bleuler's original text.[7] Indeed, it does not appear in Joseph Zinkin's competent translation of *Dementia Praecox or the Group of Schizophrenias* either. The term "thought disorder" seems to be an invention of English and American psychiatrists. For example, Eliot Slater and Martin Roth, the authors of the prestigious British textbook, *Mayer-Gross Clincal Psychiatry*, write: "When we refer to schizophrenic *thought disorder*, we mean an abnormality of the thought process . . . ; *Thought disorder* is rarely absent [in schizophrenia]; the presence of *thought disorder . . . is a diagnostic sign of the first order.*"[8] Similarly, the recent, multiauthor text, *Symptoms of Schizophrenia*, contains an entire chapter titled, "Thought Disorder." The authors state: "Thought disorder is one of the most striking clinical features of schizophrenia. . . . Advances in our knowledge about thought disorder in schizophrenia are apparent."[9]*

What did Bleuler actually say? Under the heading, "The Definition of the Disease," he stated:** "The disease is characterized by a specific type of alteration of thinking, feeling, and relation to the external world which appears nowhere else in this particular fashion."[10] For "alteration of thinking, feeling" the original German text has: "*Alteration des Denkens und Fühlens.*"[11] Thought is a noun, thinking is a gerund (verbal noun); the former implies an entity or thing, the latter, an activity or process.

As I suggested, thinking is self-conversation, a word that is not listed in English dictionaries but for which there is an exact German equivalent, namely, the term *Selbstgespräch* (*Selbst* is self, *Gespräch* is conversation). It follows that if a schizophrenic person suffers from an "alteration of thinking," and if thinking is self-conversation, then he displays the consequences of disordered self-conversation, not a "thought-disorder." How can a self-conversation, that only the self can monitor, be disordered? Clearly, it cannot be. However, it

*These two sentences offer a striking illustration of how abstractions have replaced observations in the study of persons called "schizophrenic."

**Quotations from Bleuler in English are from the translation, in German from the original text.

can be self-deceptive, making the person who engages in it the "victim" of his own pretenses and prevarications.

Because ordinary medical maladies are not diagnosed on the basis of inferences about the patient's speech pattern, Bleuler was uncomfortable with having to rely on such inferences in the case of schizophrenia. He wrote: "I consider it to be a serious defect that we are forced to deduce most of the anomalies from the oral and written productions of the patients."[12] As it happens, what Bleuler calls a "defect" is in fact an important clue to the nature of schizophrenia, namely, that the observer infers the schizophrenic's "abnormal" self-conversation from his "abnormal" conversation with others, especially psychiatrists.

Precisely what is the nature of this abnormality? "According to our present point of view," wrote Bleuler, "the distortions of speech in schizophrenia are not to be differentiated from those which occur in dreams."[13] For the English phrase "distortions of speech," the German text has "die Sprachfehler."[14] At this point Zinkin's translation could have been improved by articulating the differences between the German and English texts. Sprache is "speech." Fehler is fault. Cassell's translates "Sprachfehler" as "speech defect," "grammatical mistake."[15] In the context of schizophrenia, a better translation of Sprachfehler would be "faulty speech" or "faulty speaking."

What counts as faulty speech depends on the criterion of correct speech. Clearly, many so-called schizophrenic patients have identifiable speech patterns that may be called "deviant." However, individuals who speak with an accent that identifies them as natives of Brooklyn or Dallas, Hungary or Scotland also have identifiable speech patterns that deviate from the speech pattern of the American broadcasting industry. The point is that speech defects—whether lisping, stuttering, or wrongly accented diction— are the manifestations of the speaker's faulty use of the muscles of his mouth and tongue, not of his disordered thinking or diseased brain.

These considerations bring us back to Bleuler's view that "the distortions of speech in schizophrenia are not to be differentiated from those which occur in dreams."[16] This comparison blurs the fact that when the schizophrenic patient speaks to a psychiatrist, he is addressing another person, whereas when a person dreams, he is speaking to himself. One cannot have a "distortion of speech" or a *"Sprachfehler"* in one's dreams. No dreamer lisps, stutters, or speaks with an accent.

My point is that just as the term *Selbstgespräch* implies that talking to oneself is an ordinary, normal act, so the term *Sprachfehler* implies that the schizophrenic's speech is not as radically different from normal speech as psychiatrists maintain. Careful reading of Bleuler's entire text—and especially two remarkable passages in it—supports the impression that this is the message he wanted to convey. In the first passage, Bleuler compared schizophrenic thinking with medieval thinking: "The patterns of medieval thought afford many points of comparison with schizophrenia. During that period, too, thought processes had autistically turned away from reality . . . Homo dei in the image of mortals could just as well have been the brainchild of a modern schizophrenic."[17]

In the second passage—the concluding lines of *Dementia Praecox*—Bleuler pleaded for the schizophrenic patient's right to kill himself:

I am even taking this opportunity to state clearly that our present-day social system demands great, and entirely inappropriate cruelty from the psychiatrist in this respect. People are being forced to continue to live a life that has become unbearable for them for *valid reasons*. . . . even if a few more [patients] killed themselves—does this reason justify the fact that we *torture* hundreds of patients and *aggravate* their disease?[18]

CRAZY TALK IN A CULTURAL CONTEXT

There have always been people who talked crazy. Formerly, their behavior was viewed in religious terms and called "the gift of tongues." Today, it is viewed in medical terms and called "schizophrenese." "A well-known example [of schizophrenese] in literature," declares J. R. Smythies, a prominent British psychiatrist, "is *Finnegan's Wake*. Joyce himself was never overtly schizophrenic . . . but he must have been near enough to it to be able to write schizophrenese (which normal people find almost impossible to do)."[19] For good measure, Smythies adds: "Wittgenstein's philosophical writings exhibit [this characteristic] to a singular degree." The leap from language to lesion implicit in these assertions is based only on faith, exactly as the leap from language to holiness, implicit in glossolalia as "speaking in tongues," is based only on faith.

Speaking in Tongues

The phenomenon of people speaking in a seemingly unintelligible language has been observed in all ages and in all parts of the world.[20] In the Christian West, the practice of "speaking in tongues" goes back to the beginning of this religion. In 1 Corinthians, St. Paul refers to "the tongues of men and angels" (13:1). Glossolalia is still common in the United States, mainly among Pentecostal Protestants. Because such behavior not only expresses but also evokes intense emotions, there is virtually no neutral, semantically unprejudiced way of describing it, as the various definitions of glossolalia below illustrate.

- *Webster's:* "Ecstatic speech that is usually unintelligible to hearers and is uttered in worship services of various contemporary religious groups laying great stress on religious excitation and emotional fervor."
- *New Catholic Encyclopedia:* "[C]harisma that enables the recipient to praise God in miraculous speech."[21]
- *Psychiatric Dictionary:* "Tongue jabbering; unintelligible jargon."[22]
- *American Handbook of Psychiatry:* "[M]imicking [of] animal sounds or pronouncing meaningless neologisms."[23]
- *Comprehensive Textbook of Psychiatry / V* (in a chapter titled "Typical Signs and Symptoms of Psychiatric Illness"): "[T]he expression of a revelatory message through unintelligible words."[24]
- *New Encyclopedia Britannica:* "[A] neurotic or psychotic symptom."[25]

Thus, authorities on language, religion, and medicine either canonize this phenomenon as holy or demonize it as mad. I view both glossolalia and schizophrenese anthropologically, illustrative, respectively, of the ways "man uses language when he practices religion,"[26] and of the ways man uses language when he practices psychiatry.* Both types of speech acts are behavioral strategies to overcome an actual or perceived social inferiority. Paul's First Letter to the Corinthians expresses this view quite clearly: "For it is written, 'I will destroy the wisdom of the wise, and the cleverness of the clever I will thwart.' . . . God chose what is foolish in the world to shame the wise" (1 Corinthians 1:19—28). Accordingly,

---

*In the nineteenth century, speaking in the tongue of psychodiagnostics proved that the speaker recognized madness as a medical malady; today, it proves that mental illness is like any other illness and, specifically, that it is a brain disease.

speaking in tongues was viewed as a manifestation of being "filled with the Holy Spirit." In the Catholic Pentecostal Movement glossolalia is still recognized as "of unassailable validity . . . of the fullness of life in the spirit."[27] In contrast, a public opinion survey conducted in 1995 revealed that while 7 percent of adult Americans reported that they have spoken in tongues, 78 percent declared that speaking in tongues is "evidence of demonic possession."[28]

I want to anticipate here an objection to the analogy between glossolalia and schizophrenese, namely, that the former occurs in a ritual, socially sanctioned context, and the latter does not. The objection is invalid. Although glossolalia is now displayed only in a religious setting, that was not true in earlier days, and is so today only because outside of such a setting it is defined as madness. In the Age of Faith—when God could be found everywhere, not just in church—there was no place inappropriate for worship and there were no boundaries to the "ritual context" of glossolalia. Today, in the Age of Madness[29]—when insanity can be found everywhere, not just in the insane asylum—there are no boundaries to the psychiatric context of psychodiagnostics (and involuntary treatment). Lay persons—journalists, juries, and assorted pundits—are no less adept at making diagnoses of mental illness than are mental health professionals. Furthermore, it is precisely the ritual context of psychiatry that causes the observer to perceive a particular pattern of behavior as abnormal or psychopathological.[30]

Schizophrenia Reconsidered

Schizophrenia remains the paradigmatic metaphoric illness of modernity: a non-illness—generated by our bafflement by what the Other qua Madman says, authoritatively declared to be a disease (justifying his involuntary hospitalization and treatment).[31] So important has schizophrenia become—not only in psychiatry but in modern society as a whole—that perhaps never before in history have so many educated people wasted so much time and money as have diverse professionals squandered on studying this nonexistent illness.

Physicians have good reason for entertaining the possibility that the schizophrenic's abnormal speech is a symptom of brain disease. Certain alterations of speech are indeed attributable to diseases of the brain, for example, aphasia due to a stroke. Are alterations of speech exhibited by schizophrenics also due to brain disease? The answer must be: No. The aphasic person does not talk crazy, he has difficulty expressing himself; for example, he may recognize a familiar object but may not be able to name it. Moreover, his speech is not gibberish (although it may be difficult to understand); he does not assert a false identity (or have other delusions); and he is embarrassed by the way he speaks. For all these reasons, the aphasic person's speech is unlikely to be interpreted as a sign of madness.

The schizophrenic person, on the other hand, has no trouble expressing himself. Indeed, he is often garrulous and grandilo-quent, or dramatically silent. He is not embarrassed by his speech behavior; on the contrary, he treats it as if it were perfectly normal. These characteristics distinguish the speech of the schizophrenic person from that of the brain-damaged person and are consistent with the view that schizophrenic discourse appears to be incom-prehensible because it is vocalized self-conversation, that is, a speech act intended to be understood by the speaker, not the listener.*

There is a vast literature on language and schizophrenia which it is not my intention to review here. Suffice it to say that much of it supports my argument. For example, Nancy Andreasen, profes-sor of psychiatry at the University of Iowa, studied the speech patterns of manic, depressed, and schizophrenic patients and found that they were not different enough to be clearly distinguishable from one another. She concluded: "The practice of referring glob-ally to 'thought disorder,' as if it were homogeneous, [ought to] be avoided in the future."[32] Other investigators found that the seem-ingly senseless speech of schizophrenic subjects makes sense if the listener pays attention to the speaker's interweaving of personal material into a discourse to which it does not belong.[33]

After completing a comprehensive review of the literature on language and schizophrenia, psychologists Sherry Rochester and J. R. Martin observed: "In 1911, Bleuler reported his experience of being a confused listener in the presence of incoherent speak-ers. . . . [T]o make a statement about incoherent discourse is really to make a statement about one's own confusion as a listener."[34] Apparently unable to appreciate or acknowledge that the point of

---

*Sexual self-stimulation (masturbation), unlike copulation, is a sex act intended to involve and be enjoyed by the self only, not someone else (as well). Similarly, semantic self-stimulation (schizophrenese) is a speech act intended to involve and be understood by the self only, not someone else (as well).

the whole schizophrenia enterprise is to legitimize that alleged condition as a real disease, and the psychiatrists who treat schizophrenics as real doctors,* Rochester and Martin concluded: "The study of the language use of schizophrenia has not been a happy enterprise. Every major reviewer in the last decade has observed that there is no adequate theory of why schizophrenic speakers produce aberrant discourse."[35]

The leap from aberrant discourse to aberrant brain function—that is, the proposition that a disorder of language is *ipso facto* a disease of the brain—is plainly fallacious. Language is a form of self-expression and communication. There are many reasons why a person may express himself in unconventional ways. If we regard deviant speech as a symptom of a brain disease called "schizophrenia" (caused by a "split" between thought and language), then we ought to regard other forms of deviant self-expressions—such as painting, music, and dancing—as manifestations of brain diseases as well. Deviant painting—exemplified by the works of Pablo Picasso or Jackson Pollock—would then qualify as the symptom of the brain disease called "schizovisia" (caused by a "split" between seeing and representing).

However, asking why a schizophrenic speaker produces aberrant discourse, or why a schizovisic painter produces aberrant pictures, is asking the wrong questions. People have *reasons* for what they do, not *theories* of "producing" what others deem aberrant. Today, psychiatrists regard Coué's cure, using "healthy talk," as only slightly less aberrant.[36]**

---

*The present psychiatric focus on schizophrenia resembles Freud's focus on neurosis. The reality, frequency, and seriousness of the fictitious diseases called "neuroses" legitimized psychoanalysis as a treatment and the psychoanalysts as therapists; similarly, the reality, frequency, and seriousness of the fictitious diseases called "schizophrenia" and "depression" legitimize biological psychiatry as a medical specialty and the use of mind-altering drugs and electroshocking the brain as treatments for mental/brain diseases.

**Émile Coué (1857–1926), a French pharmacist, seized on the idea, popular in his day, that "nervous diseases" were imaginary maladies, caused by the affected person's literally talking himself into feeling sick and hence being sick. Coué reasoned that if crazy talk can make a person sick, healthy talk—that is, the patient "talking himself out" of being sick—will cure him. Accordingly, he instructed patients to ritualistically repeat to themselves the phrase: "Every day and in every way I am getting better and better." This method came to be called "autosuggestion" or "Couéism." In Europe during the early decades of this century, Couéism was one of the most popular methods of psychotherapy.

CRAZY HEARING

Because everyone talks to himself, and because sometimes people experience their thoughts as if they were voices, "hearing voices" is, and has always been, a ubiquitous phenomenon. Only after the advent of psychiatry did the phrase "hearing voices" become categorized as a pathological symptom, called "auditory hallucination."*

Hallucination: A Psychiatric Invention

Only in a psychiatric context is the term "hearing voices" interpreted as synonymous with hallucination and, as such, a symptom of serious mental illness (typically schizophrenia). At the same time, the psychiatric literature is replete with references to auditory hallucinations in normal persons. For example, in 1960, Gordon R. Forrer reported:

It has become increasingly evident that . . . hallucinatory experiences are quite common in the sane . . . These experiences are quite universally experienced; and because of their occurrence in normal people, I have chosen the term "benign hallucinations" as an indication that there is *no other accompanying psychopathology* apparent.[37]

It is revealing of the psychiatric mind-set that although this psychiatrist acknowledges that hearing voices is "universally experienced," he continues to call it "hallucination" and classifies it as a manifestation of "psychopathology."

Studies conducted by psychologists confirm the ubiquity of the experience of hearing one's own thoughts as voices. For example, 71 percent of a group of college students queried by psychologists reported that they heard voices. One respondent stated: "I am scared of driving at night and I sometimes hear something or someone telling me to slow down and take it easy." Another said: "Sometimes when I do something wrong, or am about to do something wrong, or am not doing something I am supposed to do, I hear a sweet voice from my mother telling me to do or not do it."[38]

*The *OED* traces the *nontechnical* use of the term "hallucination" to the seventeenth century.

The phrase "hearing voices" warrants a brief remark about the distinction between voice and speech. Human voice is essentially biological: It is the sound produced by means of lungs, larynx, and buccal structures. Whereas speech, which depends on the ability to produce voice, is essentially cultural: It is the language(s) a person speaks and the way he speaks. Some adjectives—for example, loud and soft—may be used to describe both voice and speech; some apply only to one or the other, for example, only voice can be low- or high-pitched, and only speech can be coherent or incoherent.

These distinctions are important because they highlight an error intrinsic to the notion of so-called command hallucination, exemplified by a person's allegedly "hearing voices" ordering him to, say, kill his wife. Such a person "hears" speech, not voices. Hence, it is an error to accept the assertion that he hears voices and to define the efforts to suppress the voices as a "treatment." It would be more useful, for both the hallucinating subject and his interlocutor, to ask the subject about the identity, characteristics, and motives of the agent who is "speaking" to him (for example, his gender, accent or dialect, motives, relationship to the listener, and so forth).

We call a normal person's attribution of his thoughts to others "projection," a term that invalidates his claim or perception. But we call a schizophrenic person's attribution of his inner speech to others "hearing voices," a term that validates his mendacity or misperception.* To be sure, a person may sincerely believe that he "hears voices," just as he may sincerely believe that he is Jesus (or some other falsehood). But just as his assertion that he is Jesus does not mean that he is the Savior, his assertion that he hears voices does not mean that he actually hears voices. Perhaps this expression is intended to mean only that his experience is exceptionally vivid, much as a pious person may report having an exceptionally vivid "religious" experience.

Actually, both Bleuler and Freud identified certain religious experiences as similar to schizophrenic symptoms. Above, I cited the passage where Bleuler compared "medieval thinking" with

---

*It is the psychiatrist's professional duty to authenticate the hallucinating person's claim that he hears voices as actually hearing voices. Validating this falsehood as fact is essential for the integrity of psychiatry as a science concerned, *inter alia*, with "testing reality."

schizophrenic thinking and concluded: "Homo Dei in the image of mortals could just as well have been the brainchild of a modern schizophrenic."[39] In a different context, Freud characterized religion as a "system of wishful illusions . . . [producing] a state of blissful hallucinatory confusion."[40]*

Some observations obtained in the course of recent neuroimaging studies of schizophrenics support the interpretations I am suggesting. Let us recall that Julian Jaynes claimed that the experience of hearing voices (auditory hallucination) is "just like hearing actual sound."[41] If that were so, the cerebral-physiological processes accompanying the hallucinating person's experience would be similar to those accompanying normal hearing; which is exactly what researchers using neuroimaging technics to study brain activation in hallucinating patients expected to find. Instead, they found changes in the region of the brain activated during speaking. "Broca's area is a surprise," commented Jerome Engel, a neurologist at the University of California at Los Angeles, "since that's where you make sounds, not where you hear them. *I would have expected more activity in Wernicke's area, which is where you hear.*"[42]

Neuroscientists do not interpret this finding as supporting the view that the person who claims to be hearing voices is disavowing his (aggressive, erotic, grandiose) thoughts. Instead, they interpret it as evidence that schizophrenia is a brain disease. Thus, P. K. McGuire and his associates continue to refer to "brain regions involved in the *production of hallucinations*,"[43] as if speech were a product of the brain, rather than of the person; speculate that their "observations are suggestive of a disruption of cortico-cortical connectivity, which is thought to be a critical feature of the neuropathology of schizophrenia;"[44] and conclude that hearing voices is "caused by a disordered monitoring of inner speech."[45]

This is a tortured interpretation. Inner speech, by definition, is not accessible (to inspection) to anyone other than the "inner" speaker. We cannot observe anyone else's inner speech. We can observe only the "outer" speech of the Other. From it, we can infer his inner speech and impart to it various interpretations. Bleuler interpreted it as the manifestation of a "thinking disorder," characteristic of schizophrenia. Contemporary psychiatrists interpret it

*Freud was inordinately fond of the word "hallucination." The Index to his collected works lists well over a hundred entries for the words "hallucination" and "hallucinatory."

as a manifestation of a "disorder of inner speech." I interpret it as a manifestation of disavowed self-conversation, projected onto imaginary "Voices." This suggestion is supported not only by the neuroimaging evidence cited, but also by the familiar clinical observation that when a (hearing) person who has auditory hallucinations is engaged in oral activity, such as eating or speaking, his imaginary voices become less noticeable or stop altogether.[46]

Varieties of "Abnormal" Voices

Hearing voices is not the only type of self-conversation which subjects describe as unwanted and often attribute to madness (mental illness). Actually, many more people complain of obsessional thoughts than of hallucinations. The description of these phenomena is systematically crippled by being couched in a psychopathological vocabulary, as the following examples illustrate.

The American Psychiatric Association's *Diagnostic and Statistical Manual* defines obsessions as:

recurrent, persistent ideas, thoughts, images, or impulses that are ego-dystonic, that is, they are not experienced as voluntarily produced, but rather as thoughts that invade consciousness and are experienced as senseless or repugnant. . . . The most common obsessions are repetitive thoughts of violence (e.g., killing one's child), contamination (e.g., becoming infected by shaking hands).[47]

A standard psychiatric text offers this example: "A young law student had the frightening thought every time he turned on the light, 'My father will die'; to allay his anxiety, he would have to touch the switch and think to himself, 'I take back that thought.'"[48] A psychology text states: "Individuals with obsessive-compulsive disorder experience obsessions (ideas or images that repeatedly seem to take over thoughts)."[49] In the first example the patient speaks of "taking back thoughts"; in the second, the experts speak of "ideas taking over thoughts." Both locutions illustrate the incoherence of this vocabulary.

The authors of a standard British textbook of psychiatry explain: "Obsessional ideas and images are disturbing and often very distressing: they may be frightening, blasphemous, disgusting or obscene. Their intrusive nature is characteristic. One patient described it as—'it is like being chained, my mind is gripped by the thoughts, . . . *I keep trying to tell my mind to forget about them, I seem to remember them all the more.*"[50]

This description illustrates the similarities between the obsessional's self-repudiated thinking and the smoker's self-repudiated smoking. In both instances (and in countless others) the subject engages in a habitual pattern of behavior, yet asserts that he would rather abstain from the behavior; each actor affirms that his problematic behavior is unwanted and beyond his control, yet bitterly resists efforts—by himself or others—to deprive him of his habit. In fact, such efforts often lead to a "worsening" of the ostensibly unwanted behavior ("symptom") and to increasingly desperate psychiatric efforts to abolish it ("treatment").* Without disapproval, the authors of a standard American psychiatric text observe: "Leukotomy [lobotomy] has been recommended by some authors as a valuable approach to the treatment of patients with obsessive-compulsive disorder."[51]

In lieu of this psychiatric perspective and vocabulary, I propose to view obsessional thoughts as instances of self-conversations—specifically, as inner dialogues whose character and contents the speaker-listener is unable or unwilling to change. Long ago, Freud correctly called attention to the similarities between the ritualized thoughts and acts of the obsessional person ("neurotic") and the ritualized thoughts and acts of the religious person ("orthodox"). The essential difference between these two sets of behaviors lies not in the minds or heads of the subject, but in the interpretation he and society place on them. Simply put, the religious ritualist performs acts of thinking and doing that he and his many coreligionists alike regard as rational and desirable, indeed holy; whereas the obsessional ritualist performs acts of thinking and doing that he as well as his family and society regard as irrational and undesirable, indeed insane.

The examples I have cited illustrate the aptness of the German term, *Gedankenlautwerden*, which Bleuler used to describe what we call "hearing voices." He wrote: "Where . . . auditory hallucinations continually dominate the clinical picture, one can practically always conclude that one is dealing with schizophrenia. The phe-

---

*The use of external coercion to change such behavior is especially likely to intensify the agent's devotion to his ceremonial-ritual habit. Ironically, we disapprove of coerced religious conversion as a violation of basic human rights, and approve of coerced psychiatric drugging as a treatment.

nomenon of thoughts being heard (*Gedankenlautwerden*) occurs only very rarely in other psychoses."[52] The translator's insertion of the German word here indicates that he recognized that the connotations of the term *Gedankenlautwerden—Denken* (thinking), *laut* (audible), and *werden* (becoming)—differ significantly from the connotations of the phrase "hearing voices." Bleuler described the patient who claims that he hears nonexistent voices as a person whose "thinking has become audible." This interpretation is consistent with the accounts given in some psychiatric textbooks written in English. For example, Eliot Slater and Martin Roth state that "many [patients] . . . speak of thoughts coming aloud," and quote a schizophrenic patient as saying: "All sorts of 'thoughts' seem to come to me, as if someone is 'speaking' them inside my head."[53] Nevertheless, English-speaking psychiatrists describe such a person as "hearing voices." In contrast, the German phrase "*Gedankenlautwerden*" describes thinking (inner speech, speaking to oneself) becoming audible.

The Power to Name: Convention and Truth in Schizophrenia

The power to name is critical in every walk of life, perhaps nowhere more than in psychiatry. It would be no exaggeration to say that the core act of the psychiatrist is the invidious naming of the Other's behavior, especially linguistic behavior. Bleuler's (mis)identification of the mental patient's refusal to speak as a characteristic symptom of schizophrenia is illustrative. He wrote: "Even patients fully capable of work may long remain mute . . . this is a frequent symptom. . . . [T]heir gaze may show us, intentionally or unintentionally, that they have heard us."[54] Instead of seeing such persons as defiant, psychiatrists see them as diseased.

The Trappist monk is silent because he chooses not to speak. The mental patient is silent because he suffers from schizophrenia, manifested by "mutism." Imprisoned in a mental hospital, Ezra Pound refused to talk to his psychiatric jailers; the doctors declared that he was displaying "retardation of verbal expression."[55] Preoccupied with searching for the mental patient's brain disease, we cannot hear his Voice, much less his Silence.

Like the psychiatrist, the psychotic too has the power to abuse language. As I already suggested, the schizophrenic patient who "hallucinates" or has "delusions" is profoundly dishonest with himself. He denies that the voices he hears are his own thoughts and that his delusions are metaphors he interprets literally. It is neither possible nor necessary to answer the question of whether the person who deceives himself is lying or not. It is possible, however, to construct an accurate account of such a person's behavior, both verbal and nonverbal, especially his communications with himself and others.

We ought to question the schizophrenic's sincerity. Why does a hallucinating person never ask himself why "the voices" command him to perform acts of cruelty rather than acts of kindness; why does the deluded person—who claims, for example, that he is Jesus—never asks himself why his mother's name is not Mary, or how Jesus learned to speak English? Bleuler recognized this element of seeming insincerity in schizophrenic delusions. Remarking about a patient who stated that "I am buried alive now"—a transparent metaphor for his languishing in an asylum—he stated: "Generally, it is very striking how many patients . . . reveal the same indifference to their own delusions, with which, however, they are constantly preoccupied."[56]

I believe viewing the schizophrenic as a liar would advance our understanding of schizophrenia. What does he lie about? Principally about his own anxieties, bewilderments, confusions, deficiencies, and self-deceptions. He pretends that he is not confused, impotent, and insignificant; he is confident, powerful, and supremely significant.

"HEARING VOICES": A CRITICAL REEXAMINATION

Modern textbooks of psychiatry treat talking to oneself as a cardinal symptom of schizophrenia and, in the process, misrepresent the phenomenon. For example, Kaplan and Sadock state: "Most common are auditory hallucinations, or the hearing of voices. . . . Frequently the voices address the patient, comment on what he is doing and what is going on around him, or are threatening or obscene and very disturbing to the patient."[57]

The hallucinating person's claim that his hallucinations are "very disturbing" cannot be accepted at face value. After all, it is the hallucinating person who produces the voices he hears. If, on balance, the voices would perturb him more than they please him, he would stop producing them. Similarly, if hallucinations were as disturbing for patients as psychiatrists say they are, patients would be eager to take the drugs that silence their "voices." However, many hallucinating persons refuse to take antipsychotic drugs voluntarily, preferring the company of their "voices" to the human voices available to them or to silence.

I might parenthetically call attention here to another important inconsistency: We regard the person who alienates his thoughts (say, about harming others) and blames them on "voices" as a victim of brain disease—a patient who deserves treatment; but we regard the person who alienates his craving (say, for cigarettes) and blames them on merchants as a victim of deceptive advertising—a plaintiff who deserves monetary compensation.

We must keep in mind that what makes "hearing voices" of psychiatric as well as legal interest is not the actor's "hallucination" itself, but the (mis)conduct in which he engages, ostensibly at the command of his voices. The person who complains of hearing voices, or acts as if he were listening to an absent person while someone is speaking to him, is violating social convention. An adult who blames his own bad thoughts on "voices" resembles a young child who blames his misconduct on an innocent sibling or imaginary stranger. The adult world easily sees through the child's naive stratagem, perhaps because children are not subject to the same legal punishments as adults. In contrast, the adult world, represented by the combined prestige of law, psychiatry, and the media, feels compelled to accept the "psychotic" adult's similar stratagem—that he actually hears voices which he is powerless to resist—to avoid having to treat the offending person as a responsible moral agent.[58]*

The collusion between the psychotic and the psychiatrist is necessary for the protection of their respective constructions of reality. Both transform acts into happenings. The patient does it by denying that his (mis)behavior is an implementation of his own will; instead, he defines himself as a slave who obediently carries out the commands of the Voices that are his Masters. The psychiatrist does it by denying that the patient is a moral agent who acts;

*Hearing, listening, and obeying have a common etymological root in the Latin, *oboedire* or *obaudire* ("toward" and "to listen"). Mental patients have "command hallucinations"; normal people remind themselves of their resolutions.

instead, he defines the patient—by using psychiatric jargon or the passive voice—as a helpless victim of pathological processes in his brain. Declares Anthony Clare, professor of psychiatry at Trinity College in Dublin: "Some patients may deny hallucinations. . . . Careful analysis may subsequently reveal that such people are *in fact auditorily hallucinated.*"[59] That, of course, is impossible. Listening to a message—whether to the words of another person or one's own thoughts—requires minding it. That is why the proverbial absent-minded scientist—seemingly listening to his wife but actually thinking about his work—cannot hear what she is saying to him; and why she aptly complains that he is "not listening" to her. If the hallucinating person hears voices, it is because he listens to them.

Bleuler recognized this. Noting that schizophrenics often enjoy hearing and talking to their "voices," he wrote: "The 'voices' are the means by which the megalomaniac realizes his wishes, the religiously preoccupied achieves his communication with God and the Angels."[60] Moreover, Bleuler often used the word "voices" metaphorically, to refer to the patient's own thoughts. Why has this locution become literalized? Why do psychiatrists and people generally believe that crazy people actually hear nonexistent voices?

The answer, I believe, is that the image of "hearing voices" faithfully reflects the alienation-plus-rejection-of-responsibility, by both patient and doctor, that we regard as a fundamental feature of the condition we call "schizophrenia." The dynamic of this collusion and double alienation is not difficult to reconstruct. The patient feels alienated from his own thoughts.* Why? Because he does not want to be responsible for them. Hiding behind the excuse of slavishly obeying a Higher Law, he declares: "I heard God's voice ordering me to kill my wife." Self-alienation enables the patient to reject responsibility for his behavior.

Mutatis mutandis, the psychiatrist and the society whose interests he represents feel alienated from the patient. Why? Because they do not want to treat the schizophrenic as a responsible person. Alienating the Other enables them to deprive him of

---

*The claim of hearing voices need not be a manifestation of alienation. The homeless person who tells a psychiatrist that God is talking to him may be only trying to obtain room and board in a mental hospital, a service he cannot secure by asking for it.

responsibility for his behavior. Hiding behind the excuse of sensibly obeying the "voice" of Medical Science, the psychiatrist declares: "The patient is ill and is dangerous to himself or others." The law and society support this fateful collusion between mad-man and mad-doctor, generating a steady stream of tragic assaults and murders—by so-called hallucinating mental patients—that go unpunished.[61]

MENTAL TREATMENT: MODERNITY'S MASTER METAPHOR

There remains for us to consider one of the most curious contradictions in the modern literature on the mind, namely, that even theoreticians of the mind who deny its existence affirm the reality of its diseases and support the coercive psychiatric practices such diseases allegedly justify; and that even the clinicians who deny the existence of mental disease affirm the reality of mental treatments for them.

There is no great mystery about the basic reason for this stubborn inconsistency. It lies in the transformation of the soul into the mind-brain and of the cure of souls into the treatment of minds-as-brains. More than a century ago, Søren Kierkegaard (1813–1855) identified the phenomenon thus:

In our time it is the physician who exercises the cure of souls. . . . The demoniacal has been regarded therapeutically. As a matter of course: *"Mit Pulver und mit Pillen"* [With powders and with pills]. . . . The therapeutic way of viewing the case regards the phenomena as purely physical.[62]

In our time, the Argentinean novelist Adolfo Bioy Casares restated this insight in more modern terms:

Well then, maybe it would be worth mentioning the three periods of history. When man believed that happiness was dependent upon God, he killed for religious reasons. When man believed that happiness was dependent upon the form of government, he killed for political reasons. After dreams that were too long, true nightmares . . . we arrived at the present period of history. Man woke up, discovered that which he always knew, that happiness is dependent upon health, and began to kill for therapeutic reasons.[63]

Philosophers

Many modern moral philosophers assert that the word "mind" is a stand-in for the person as moral agent; yet, they treat persons called "mental patients" as nonagents.

In his celebrated Gifford Lectures for 1953–1954—published in two volumes, *The Self as Agent* and *Persons in Relation*[64]—John Macmurray identifies the mind as a term we use to describe various activities of the self or person. He then offers the following account of the ubiquitous conflict between desire and reason:

Attempts to describe the relation between these [warring] elements in the Self tend to deny the unity which they seek to analyse, by lending to the parts the characters which properly belong only to the whole. The one Self becomes two selves—a higher self and a lower self, a controlling self and a self that is to be controlled.[65]

This view implies that mental illness is not a literal (bodily) illness but a type of wrong-minding. Nevertheless, Macmurray accepts the psychiatric doctrine that such a moral struggle constitutes a "diagnosable medical disease." He writes: "The practice of psychotherapy involves a relation between a doctor and patient in which the doctor has to *diagnose a disease*. . . . The patient's *illness* consists in the fact that his conscious purposes are systematically thwarted by features of his behaviour which he is unable to control."[66]

Instead of scrutinizing the psychiatrist's power, Macmurray tacitly supports it: He treats the patient as irrational, the therapist as rational, and declares: "[The] distinction between Self and Other . . . [is] the basis of rational (or irrational) behavior. We need not settle this issue [of rationality], which must be left to the psychologists."[67] Then he offers this hypothetical vignette:

[A student is visiting his psychology professor] to consult him about the progress of his work. The interview begins as a simple personal conversation between them . . . As it proceeds, however, it becomes evident that something is wrong with the pupil. He is in an abnormal state of mind, and the psychologist recognizes clear symptoms of hysteria. At once the attitude of the teacher changes. He becomes a professional psychologist, observing and dealing with a classifiable case of mental disorder.[68]

Suppose that instead of the psychologist noticing the abnormal behavior of his pupil, the pupil notices the abnormal behavior of his professor. Could the pupil restructure the relationship, treating the teacher as an alcoholic? Hardly.

In his 1957 Gifford lectures, *Freedom of the Will*, Austin Farrer goes over much the same ground that Macmurray covered, flirts with denying the possibility of diseased minds, only to stop short. He writes:

Turning from medicine to psychiatry, we may too readily assume that the same relationship obtains—that an art of healing, with modest preten- sions, rests upon an exact science, with independent access to the matter of its study. But in the case of mental healing, there is no such exact science. . . . Thus we find him [the psychiatrist] working with speculative and largely mythical theories, of which the verification lies in the success of the healing art, and in nothing else.[69]

Although Farrer rejects the analogy between bodily disease and mental disease, he concludes: "The believer in freedom will prob- ably wish to say that mental or emotional sickness of any kind reduces liberty . . . and that the psychiatrist works upon compulsive conditions, for the purpose of eliminating them, and restoring freedom."[70] Farrer does here precisely what Macmurray warned against, that is, he interprets the subject's experience as caused by, and the result of, a (compulsive) *condition*, rather than as the expression of the agent's self-inhibition. Farrer, too, avoids con- fronting the problems posed by psychiatric power.

Behaviorists and Psychiatric Critics

John B. Watson, the founder of behaviorism, and B. F. Skinner, its most prominent spokesman, both denied the existence of the mind. Nevertheless, both supported the use of psychiatric power based on psychiatric diagnosis.[71]

In 1913, Watson declared that there is no thought and no mind: *"What the psychologists have hitherto called thought is in short nothing but talking to ourselves."*[72] Logically, this view demanded that he view mental illness as a metaphor. Instead, he embraced the psychiatric fashion of defining social deviance as mental disease and supported psychiatric practices, the more coercive the better.

Eager to enlist psychology as a servant of psychiatry, Watson praised the psychodiagnostic enterprise and endorsed involuntary mental hospitalization: "In many . . . psychopathological disorders

. . . there are no organic disturbances of sufficient gravity to account for personality disturbance. . . . And yet the individual has a sick personality . . . [and] we have to commit him temporarily or permanently."[73] Citing two vignettes of persons whom he called "floating wrecks," he observed: "Both of these individuals have diseased personalities as ravaging in their effects as tuberculosis and cancer. But it is futile to hunt for any organic disturbance."[74] Watson advocated forcibly "retraining" such persons, like we train "the infant to reach for candy and to withdraw his hand from a candle flame."[75]

Evidently, the idea of using force to make people behave better had great appeal for Watson and he imagined to have found support for it in "behaviorist psychology," which he defined as "a purely objective experimental branch of natural science . . . [whose] goal is the prediction and *control* of behavior."[76] One can only marvel at Watson's cavalier disregard for the familiar fact that while we need knowledge to give us control over inanimate matter, we need power to give us control over people. Not surprisingly, Watson wanted to hitch the wagon of behaviorism to the oxen of institutional psychiatry, supplementing the repertoire of traditional psychiatric coercions with coercions rationalized on behavioristic grounds. He wrote:

Analysis based upon behavioristic principles is here to stay and is a necessary profession in society—to be placed upon a par with internal medicine and surgery. . . . This will be the equivalent of diagnosis. Combined with this will go *unconditioning* and then *conditioning.* These will constitute the *curative* side. . . . Behaviorism ought to be a science that prepares men and women . . . to bring up their own children in a healthy way.[77]

Enthralled by Rousseau's beatific vision of an ideally harmonious social order, and foreshadowing its brutal execution by modern totalitarian leaders, Watson dreamt of "a universe . . . free of foolish customs and conventions which have no significance in themselves." In that utopian society, children will be taught "better ways of living and thinking . . . and in turn bring up their children in still a more scientific way, until the world finally becomes a place fit for human habitation."[78]

Skinner was a devout materialist and reductionist, a belief he supported by preaching the doctrine that freedom and responsibility were illusions due to ignorance. "The hypothesis that man is not free," he explained in *Science and Human Behavior*, "is essential to the application of the scientific method to the study of human behavior. The free inner man who is held responsible . . . is only a prescientific substitute for the kinds of causes which are discovered in the course of scientific analysis."[79]

Skinner disposed of every important legal, moral, and political problem by calling it a "spurious question": "'Who *should* control?' is a spurious question"[80]; and again: "The question Who will control? is not to be answered with a proper name or by describing a kind of person (e.g., a benevolent dictator)."[81] Equally crucial to Skinnerian psychology is the absence of intentionality. He wrote: "I did not direct my life. . . . I never made decisions. Things always came up and made them for me."[82] For a man who prided himself on the design of his experiments, that was an odd thing to say.

Responsibility is an illusion, the symptom of a faulty way of speaking: "To say that a person is 'held responsible' for an act is simply to say that he is usually punished for it."[83] "'Thinking' often means 'behaving weakly' . . . Usually, however, the term refers to completed behavior which occurs on a scale so small that it cannot be detected by others."[84] Finally, Skinner supported psychiatric coercions justified by psychiatric diagnoses and called oppression in a "clinical" setting "operant therapy."[85]

Lastly, I want to say a few words about the many persons engaged in the practice of mental healing—called "clinicians" or "therapists"—who reject the existence of mental illnesses but nevertheless categorize their relations to clients as genuine treatments.

For example, R. D. Laing supported my contention that schizophrenia is not an illness, yet claimed to have developed a superior method for treating "it," in his version of an insane asylum, called Kingsley Hall.[86] Similarly, the Italian (anti)psychiatrist Franco Basaglia agreed that mental illnesses do not exist and urged that mental hospitals be abolished, yet advocated that psychiatrists treat mental patients—voluntarily or involuntarily—in medical hospitals.[87]

Other "therapists"—for example, addiction therapists, art therapists, dance therapists, dialogic therapists, group therapists, hypnotherapists, logotherapists, marriage therapists, narrative therapists, sex therapists—endorse the view that the problems their clients present are not diseases, yet insist that their interventions are treatments.[88] All these mental healers worship the word "clinical," the term that authenticates them as "therapists," defines their work site as a "clinical setting," and transforms their conversation with persons denominated as "patients" from talking-and-listening into "treatment."

CONCLUSION

As we have seen, philosophers and psychologists recoil from pushing the idea of the nonexistence of the mind to its logical conclusion and refrain from insisting on the nonexistence of mental diseases as well. Similarly, critics of psychiatry and practicing therapists recoil from pushing the idea of the nonexistence of mental illnesses to its logical conclusion and refrain from insisting on the nonexistence of mental treatments as well.

Why this is so must remain a matter of speculation. The theoreticians' reluctance is probably due to their recognition that the very existence of the mental health professions—and of other important social institutions and practices supported by them—rests on a belief in the reality of diseases attributed to the "mind" and their unwillingness to undermine so formidable an edifice. The practitioners' reluctance is probably attributable to a simpler motive, namely, economic and existential self-interest.

"If God did not exist," ventured Voltaire, "it would be necessary to invent him." *Mutatis mutandis*, we find it necessary to invent the mind, mental maladies, and mental remedies. The result is a cultural situation which W. H. Auden characterized thus:

What is peculiar and novel to our age is that . . . in all technologically advanced countries today, whatever political label they give themselves, their policies have, essentially, the same goal: to guarantee to every member of society, as a psychophysical organism, the right to physical and mental health.[89]

Epilogue: The Person as Moral Agent

It seems likely that once pre-human beings became "human," they began to observe and form an understanding of themselves. Intuitively, we regard this effort at self-observation and self-understanding as intrinsic to what we mean by being human. Less obviously, the effort to understand ourselves merges into the effort to understand human nature or the Mind.

Before long, the tendency toward role-specialization, inherent in the social nature of human life, led to certain persons becoming accredited as experts in understanding Man (*psyche*, soul, mind). The first authorities, called "priests," were soon followed by philosophers and playwrights. From antiquity until the end of the eighteenth century, the members of these three groups were the acknowledged experts on human nature. Attributed to divine sources, the authority of the priesthood was unquestioned and unquestionable and was inseparable from the authority of the "state" (as the executive arm of the "church").

With the advent of modernity, the authority of Religion to legitimize the state in general and social sanctions in particular gradually declined and was replaced by the authority of Reason. We call the result of this metamorphosis the Enlightenment and attribute its authority to Science. By the end of the nineteenth century, moral-philosophical explanations of personal conduct were thus replaced by psychological and sociological explanations of it. Today, the familiar psychoanalytic psychobabble, parading as psychological science, is being refurbished with so-called neuro-philosophical accounts of mind-as-brain. As a result, the study of man as moral agent became "unscientific" and unfashionable and was replaced by the "scientific" study of man as (mental) patient whose behavior is determined by the chemicals in his brain and the genes in his body. The moral-philosopher thus ceded his mandate to the expert in neuroscience; respect, justice, and the rule of law were replaced by compassion, tort litigation, and medical ethics; and the Welfare State was absorbed into the Therapeutic State.

Not surprisingly, the results still fall short of utopia. It is one thing to understand the structure of DNA or control a dog in a kennel. It is a very different thing to understand human behavior, much less control a person possessing rights in a society ostensibly committed to respecting "human rights." As I show, the modern expert's inability or unwillingness to concede this difference is regularly accompanied by his inability or unwillingness to acknowledge the conceptual primacy of the person as moral agent (that is, the cognitive absurdity and moral impropriety of reducing a person to his body or mind or soul).

I dare say there is something bizarre about the materialist-reductionist's denial of persons. To be sure, brains in craniums exist; and so do persons in societies. The material substrates of a human being—a person—are organs, tissues, cells, molecules, atoms, and subatomic particles. The material substrates of a human artifact—say a wedding ring—are crystals, atoms, electrons in orbits, and so forth. Scientists do not claim to be able to explain the economic or emotional value of a wedding ring by identifying its material composition; nor do they insist that a physicalistic account of its structure is superior to a cultural and personal account of its meaning. Yet, many scientists, from physicists to neurophysiologists, claim that they can explain choice and responsibility by identifying its material substrate—that "life can be explained in terms of ordinary physics and chemistry."[1] Indeed, in recent decades the canons of respectable scholarship and respectable journalism alike have virtually mandated that we view *only* biological-reductionist explanations of human behavior as scientific. The following statement, by Steven Weinberg—a Nobel Laureate and professor of physics at the University of Texas—is typical:

There are no principles of psychology that are free-standing, in the sense that they do not need *ultimately to be understood* through the study of the human brain, which in turn must *ultimately be understood* on the basis of physics and chemistry. . . . Of course, everything is *ultimately* quantum-mechanical; the question is whether quantum mechanics will appear directly in the *theory of the mind*, and not just in the deeper-level theories like chemistry on which the *theory of the mind will be based*.[2]

Socrates' dialogues—called "elenctic" (from the Greek *elenchus*, meaning to refute)—epitomize rational skepticism aimed at questioning a widely held misconception. The inexcusable conceit of the contemporary debate about the mind is that, *a priori*, it illegitimizes such skepticism. Dismissively, Weinberg writes: "[M]any of our fellow citizens still think that George [a hypothetical actor] behaves the way he does because he has a soul that is governed by laws quite unrelated to those that govern particles or thunderstorms. But let that pass."[3] My aim in this book has been to prevent such reductionism from passing as self-evident.

[handwritten margin note: What is this bracketing fad all about?]

In view of the postwar popularity of "atheistic" existentialism, it is surprising that many scientists continue to maintain that viewing a person as a responsible agent is tantamount to believing that he has a soul (that, moreover, governs his behavior). Nevertheless, the acceptance of this canard—illustrated by Weinberg's remark, which could easily be multiplied—has become *de rigueur* in current debates about the mind.

Neither Camus nor Sartre can be accused of believing in the existence of souls (in the sense in which medieval churchmen believed in them or, for that matter, in any other sense). In fact, both—albeit in very different ways—fought tirelessly to restore agency, liberty, and responsibility to the human being as person. "[T]he aim of a life," declared Camus, "can only be to increase the sum of freedom and responsibility to be found in every man and in the world. It cannot, under any circumstances, be to reduce or suppress that freedom, even temporarily."[4] Sartre was equally emphatic that we must view the person as a responsible agent. Apropos of the situation of the draftee conscripted into fighting a war he considers evil, Sartre wrote: "I deserve it [my fate] because I could always get out of it by suicide or by desertion. . . . For lack of getting out of it, I have chosen it."[5] Sartre dismissed the objection that "I did not ask to be born" with the rejoinder: "I am responsible for everything, in fact, except for my very responsibility, for I am not the foundation of my being."[6]

It is ironic that the atheists Camus and Sartre adhered to the classic Judeo-Christian view of man as a morally responsible being more faithfully than do the representatives of modern Judaism and Christianity. I believe they could do so with relative ease because, unlike the Jewish and Christian clergy, they rejected the modern medicalized abhorrence of suicide and its attribution to mental illness.[7] In fact, Sartre explicitly spurned the metaphors of psychiatry and psychoanalysis as semantic tricks for lifting the burden of freedom-as-responsibility from our shoulders. In one of the pithiest and most incisive criticisms of Freud, Sartre wrote: "Thus psychoanalysis substitutes for the notion of bad faith, the idea of a lie without a liar."[8] Bad faith is Sartre's term for self-deception, the "I" lying to the "me." "If we reject the language and the materialist mythology of psychoanalysis," Sartre continued, "we are compelled to admit that the censor must *choose*, and in order to choose must be aware of so doing."[9]

Fundamental to Sartre's perceptive analysis is the twinned idea of truth-lie. But what is truth? The word has two different uses-and-meanings. One is pragmatic: truth is what works best. The other is social: truth is what convention legitimizes as factual. As human history, especially the history of religion, tells us, the word "truth" is a dangerously intolerant term. It allows no disagreement: Who can be against the Truth? The word "understanding" is more hospitable and tolerant. It implies a dialectic and the possibility of mis-understanding. "Understanding," Michael Oakeshott observed, "is not such that we either enjoy it or lack it altogether. . . . To be human and to be aware is to encounter only what is in some manner understood."[10]

In other words, everyone, at all times, has some understanding of everything in his life. At the same time, just as every person's fingerprint is different from every other person's, so every person's understanding of himself and the world is different from every other person's. This virtually limitless variety of personal insights and outlooks is why society rightly values agreement and harmony more highly than accuracy and disputation. "An ounce of loyalty," Arthur Koestler aptly remarked, "is worth a pound of brains."

The proverb, "When in Rome, do as the Romans do," reminds us that social cooperation requires compliance with custom. In real life—the scientific enterprise included—only the legitimate can be right. Illegitimate behavior, by definition, is behavior that society deems wrong and stigmatizes as either crime or mental illness. An illegitimate idea, spoken or written, is a type of behavior, which society treats similarly.* For illegitimate ideas—be they delusions or discoveries—the only safe domain is the mind as the dialogue within.

*I believe this is why some creative persons—Mark Twain and Franz Kafka, for example—have withheld some or all of their works from publication during their lifetimes (and instructed their executors to destroy their unpublished works). These considerations also help to dispel the seemingly mysterious—but actually socially constructed—connections between genius and madness.

Notes

CHAPTER 1

1. Plato, *Theaetetus*, in *The Collected Dialogues of Plato*, pp. 895–896.

2. H. Bloom, quoted in "Bloom and doom." *Newsweek*, October 10, 1994.

3. K. Kraus, quoted in T. S. Szasz, *Anti-Freud*, p. 154. I made a small change in the translation.

4. H. Keller, *The Story of My Life*, p. 34.

5. A. Sullivan, "Letter, June 2, 1887," in H. Keller, *The Story of My Life*, p. 282.

6. A. Sullivan, "Letter, June 12, 1887," ibid., p. 285, emphasis added.

7. J. A. Macy, "A Supplementary Account of Helen Keller's Life and Education," in H. Keller, *The Story of My Life*, p. 246.

8. See chapter 6.

9. M. Twain, "Some remarks on the science of onanism" [1879], in M. Twain, *The Mammoth Cod*, p. 23; quoted from T. S. Szasz, *Sex By Prescription*, pp. 61–62.

10. J. Gleick, *Genius*, pp. 223–224.

11. Ibid., p. 224, emphasis in the original.

12. V. Woolf, *The Letters of Virginia Woolf*, vol. 4, p. 180.

13. Quoted in A. H. Bond, *Who Killed Virginia Woolf?*, p. 70.

14. V. Woolf, *The Diary of Virginia Woolf*, vol. 1, p. 6.

15. Ibid., p. 195.

16. V. Woolf, *Moments of Being*, pp. 80–81.

17. J. Lehmann, *Virginia Woolf and the World*, p. 14.

18. V. Woolf, *The Letters of Virginia Woolf*, vol. 6, p. 485. Also, L. Woolf, *The Journey Not the Arrival Matters*, p. 93.

19. L. Woolf, *The Journey*, pp. 93–94.

20. See chapter 6.

21. V. Woolf, *The Writer's Diary*, p. 165; quoted in L. Woolf, *Downhill All the Way*, p. 54.

22. A. N. Sokolov, *Inner Speech and Thought*, p. 91, emphasis in the original.

23. L. Miller, "Faith in God at heavenly heights," *USA Today*, December 21, 1994, p. D1.

24. K. L. Woodward, "Angels," *Newsweek*, December 27, 1993, pp. 52–57. See also R. Hauck, ed., *Angels;* and E. E. Freeman, *Angelic Healing*.

25. S. Burnham, quoted in K. L. Woodward, "Angels," note 24 in this chapter, p. 57.

26. A. Guip, "Bearer of good tidings," *Time*, December 27, 1993, p. 61.

27. This and subsequent biblical citations are from the Authorized King James Version.

28. Genesis 3:4.

29. 1 John 3:8.

30. Job 1:9.

31. Matthew 4:3–4.

32. Quoted in G. C. Morgan, *The Voice of the Devil*, p. 26.

33. In this connection, see S. Milgram, *Obedience to Authority*.

34. See T. S. Szasz, *Ceremonial Chemistry* and *Our Right to Drugs*.

35. For further discussion, see chapter 5.

36. A. Bierce, "The Matter of Manner" [1899], in A. Bierce, *Poems of Ambrose Bierce*, p. 133.

37. M. M. Bakhtin, *Dialogic Imagination*, pp. 349–350, emphasis in the original.

38. T. S. Szasz, *The Second Sin*, p. 113.

39. For a more detailed discussion of "crazy talk" and "crazy hearing," see chapter 6.

40. D. L. Rosenhan and M.E.P. Seligman, *Abnormal Psychology*, p. 237, emphasis added.

41. For further discussion of the mind as God, see chapter 5.

42. A. Storr, *Solitude*, p. 81.

43. C. Morris, *The Discovery of the Individual, 1050–1200*, p. 2. See generally, T. S. Szasz, *Cruel Compassion*, chapter 5.

44. G. W. McClure, *Sorrow and Consolation in Italian Humanism*, p. 13.

45. Ibid., p. 20, emphasis added.

46. Ibid., pp. 20, 51.

47. Montaigne, M. de, quoted in M. A. Screech, *Montaigne and Melancholy*, p. 69.

48. Ibid., p. 68.

49. R. Hausheer, "Introduction," in I. Berlin, *Against the Current*, p. xxxi.

50. I. Kant, "Vom Erkenntnisvermögen" ("Power to Know"), in *I. Kant*, vol. 11, pp. 465, 500, emphasis added; the translation is mine.

51. F. M. Müller, *The Science of Thought*, pp. 57.

52. Ibid., pp. 202–203, 573–574.

53. M. M. Bakhtin, *Speech Genres*, p. 68.

54. D. L. Rosenhan, "On being sane in insane places," *Science* 179: 250–258, 1973; emphasis added.

55. Ibid., p. 69.

56. A. N. Sokolov, *Inner Speech and Thought*, p. 92.

57. F. M. Müller, *The Science of Thought*, p. 118.

58. M. M. Bakhtin, *Speech Genres*, p. 127.

CHAPTER 2

1. See, for example, D. Goleman, "A genetic clue to bed-wetting is located," *New York Times*, July 1, 1995, p. 8.

2. M. Oakeshott, *On Human Conduct*, p. 15.

3. See chapter 4.

4. See generally J. Kleinig, *Paternalism*; and R. Sartorius, ed., *Paternalism*.

5. M. Polanyi, *Personal Knowledge*, p. 405.

6. "Pope's letter: A 'sinister' world has led to 'crimes against life,'" *New York Times*, March 31, 1995, p. A12.

7. See chapter 5.

8. J. Butler, *Butler's Fifteen Sermons*, p. 31. See also E. Sprague, "Butler, Joseph," in P. Edwards, ed., *The Encyclopedia of Philosophy*, vols. 1–2, pp. 432–434.

9. Ibid., pp. 148, 156.

10. A. S. Kaufman, "Responsibility, Moral and Legal," in P. Edwards, ed., *The Encyclopedia of Philosophy*, vol. 7, p. 188.

11. F. A. Hayek, *The Constitution of Liberty*, p. 75.

12. C. S. Lewis, *The Business of Heaven*, p. 52, emphasis in the original.

13. E. N. de C. Andrade, *Isaac Newton*, p. 19, emphasis added. See also, P. Beckman, *A History of PI*.

14. See S. Milgram, *Obedience to Authority*.

15. Voltaire, "Freedom of Thought," in Voltaire, *Philosophical Dictionary*, pp. 355–356.

16. T. S. Szasz, "The communication of distress between child and parent," *British Journal of Medical Psychology*, 32 (1959) 161–170.

17. W. Shakespeare, *Measure for Measure*, 2.2.163.

18. See T. S. Szasz, *Ceremonial Chemistry* and *Our Right to Drugs*.

19. Quoted in "Losing their minds in Bogota," *World Press Review* (October 1994), pp. 20–21.

20. J. Milton, *Paradise Lost*, Book 3, lines 124–128.

21. See chapter 6.

22. B. Williams, "The Idea of Equality," in J. Feinberg, ed., *Moral Concepts*, pp. 153–171; p. 158.

23. Ibid., pp. 158, 160.

24. T. S. Szasz, *The Second Sin*, p. 47.

25. A. S. Kaufman, "Responsibility, Moral and Legal," in P. Edwards, ed., *The Encyclopedia of Philosophy*, vol. 7: 183–188; p. 183.

26. L. Noel, *Intolerance*, p. 143.

27. See T. S. Szasz, *The Manufacture of Madness* and *Ceremonial Chemistry*.

28. See T. S. Szasz, *Ceremonial Chemistry*.

29. W. Shakespeare, *King Lear* 1.2.115–123.

30. T. S. Szasz, "Idleness and lawlessness in the Therapeutic State," *Society* 32 (May-June 1995); 30–35.

31. For example, see J. Maritain, *Moral Philosophy*.

32. J. C. Traupman, *The New College Latin & English Dictionary*, p. 465; see also H. C. Black, *Black's Law Dictionary*.

33. See R. Abelson and K. Nielsen, "Ethics, History of," in P. Edwards, ed., *The Encyclopedia of Philosophy*, vol. 3, p. 85.

34. See T. S. Szasz, *Insanity* and *Cruel Compassion*.

35. W. Blackstone, *Commentaries on the Laws of England*, pp. 211–212.

36. W. Shakespeare, *Hamlet* 2.2.547–550.

37. Ibid., 5.2.219–226.

38. J. Orieux, *Voltaire*, p. 84.

39. See T. S. Szasz, *Our Right to Drugs*.

40. S. E. Sprott, *The English Debate on Suicide*, p. 112, emphasis added.

41. W. Blackstone, op. cit., p. 212.

42. I. Berlin, "Historical Inevitability" [1953], in I. Berlin, *Four Essays on Liberty*, pp. 41–117; pp. 115-116; see also F. A. Hayek, *The Counter-Revolution of Science*.

43. See T. S. Szasz, *Cruel Compassion*, chapter 6; and *A Lexicon of Lunacy*, chapter 11.

44. R. J. Werblowsky and J. Wigoder, eds., *The Encyclopedia of the Jewish Religion*, p. 367; see also J. Goldin, ed., *The Living Talmud*, pp. 40, 154.

45. See chapter 4.

CHAPTER 3

1. J. A. Macy, "A Supplementary Account of Helen Keller's Life and Education," in H. Keller, *The Story of My Life*, p. 246.

2. C. R. Barclay and P. A. DeCooke, "Ordinary, Everyday Memories: Some of the Things of Which Selves are Made," in U. Neisser and E. Winograd, eds., *Remembering Reconsidered*, pp. 93, 92.

3. J. R. Searle, "The mystery of consciousness," *New York Review of Books*, November 2, 1995, pp. 60–66; p. 62, emphasis added.

4. F. H. Frankel, "Discovering new memories in psychotherapy—childhood revisited, fantasy, or both?" *New England Journal of Medicine* 333 (1995): 591–594.

5. S. Begley, "You must remember this: How the brain forms 'false memories'," *Newsweek*, September 26, 1994, pp. 68–69.

6. B. L. Bugelski, "Memory," in R. J. Corsini, ed., *Encyclopedia of Psychology*, vol. 2, pp. 354–356; p. 356.

7. J. Kotre, *White Gloves*.

8. See, B. L. Bugelski, "Memory," in R. J. Corsini, ed., *Encyclopedia of Psychology*, vol. 2, pp. 354–356; see also, P. J. Hilts, *Memory's Ghost*.

9. M. Oakeshott, *Experience and Its Modes*, p. 93.

10. G. H. Mead, *The Philosophy of the Present*, pp. 29, 31, emphasis added.

11. L. Carroll, *Through the Looking Glass* [1872], quoted in *Bartlett's Familiar Quotations*, edited by J. Kaplan, 16th ed., p. 519.

12. E. Winograd, "Continuities Between Ecological and Laboratory Approaches to Memory," in U. Neisser and E. Winograd, eds., op. cit., p. 17.

13. Ibid.

14. The story of the Australian writer Helen Darville is a dramatic example; see P. Shenon, "For fiction, and fibbing, she takes the prize," *New York Times*, September 26, 1995, p. A4.

15. F. A. Yates, *The Art of Memory*, p. 4.

16. Quoted in ibid., p. 29, emphasis added.

17. Quoted in ibid., p. 86.

18. D. Goleman, "Studying the secrets of childhood memory: Researchers find recollection may be linked to language," *New York Times*, April 6, 1993, pp. C1, C11.

19. Quoted in M. A. Screech, *Montaigne and Melancholy*, p. 90.

20. M. Twain, quoted in A. B. Paine, *Mark Twain*, vol. 3, p. 1269.

21. J. T. McQuiston, "Suspect in LIRR shooting says eyewitnesses are racists," *New York Times*, January 27, 1995, pp. B1, B5; "Shooting victim and defendant go eye to eye in courtroom," ibid., January 28, 1995, pp. 21, 24.

22. See J. E. Mack, *Abduction*.

23. E. Winograd, "Ecological and Laboratory Approaches to Memory," in U. Neisser and E. Winograd, eds., op. cit., p. 18.

24. J. P. Hilts, *Memory's Ghost*, p. 100. Most of my comments about H. M. are based on Hilts's account.

25. Ibid., p. 100.

26. Ibid., p. 97.

27. Ibid., p. 99.

28. Ibid., p. 107.

29. Ibid., p. 119.

30. Ibid., p. 121.

31. Ibid., p. 146.

32. Ibid., p. 231.

33. F. Kafka, "In the Penal Colony," in F. Kafka, *The Penal Colony*, p. 198.

34. S. L. Hostler, J. H. Allaire, and R. A. Christoph, "Childhood sexual abuse reported by facilitated communication," *Pediatrics* 91 (1993): 1190–1191.

35. D. L. Wheeler, J. W. Jacobson, R. A. Paglieri, and A. A. Schwartz, "An experimental assessment of facilitated communication," *Mental Retardation* 31 (1993): 49–59 and W. LaRue, "Under fire: PBS takes critical look at SU professor's controversial technique," *Syracuse Herald-Journal*, October 19, 1993, pp. D1, D3.

36. M. Prior and R. Cummins, "Questions about facilitated communication and autism," *Journal of Autism and Developmental Disorders* 22 (1992): 331–337, pp. 335, 336.

37. See S. Bettison, "Informal evaluation of Crossley's facilitated communication," *Journal of Autism and Developmental Disorders* 22 (1992): 561–562; D. Biklen, "Communication unbound: Autism and praxis," *Harvard Educational Review* 60 (1991): 291–314; D. Biklen, "Typing to talk: Facilitated communication," *American Journal of Speech and Language Pathology* 1 (1992): 15-17, 21–22; L. Jaroff, "Lies of the mind," *Time*, November 29, 1993, pp. 52–59; and J. Berger, "Shattering the silence of autism: Parents say treatment to help children communicate is a delusionary sham," *New York Times*, February 12, 1994, pp. 21, 27.

38. D. L. Wheeler, J. W. Jacobson, R. A. Paglieri, and A. A. Schwartz, "An experimental assessment of facilitated communication," *Mental Retardation* 31 (1993): 49–59 pp. 49, 58, emphasis added.

39. D. Goleman, "Miscoding mixes memory: Distortions are tied to brain's storage system," *International Herald-Tribune*, June 2, 1994, p. 10.

40. See C. Mackay, *Extraordinary Popular Delusions and the Madness of Crowds*; and T. S. Szasz, *The Manufacture of Madness*.

41. See G. Alexander, "Big Mother: The state's use of mental health experts in dependency cases," *Pacific Law Journal* 24, pp. 1465-1496 (April), 1993; H. Wakefield and R. Underwager, "Recovered memories of alleged sexual abuse: Lawsuits against parents," *Behavioral Sciences and the Law* 10: 483–507, p. 1992; and L. Jaroff, "Lies of the mind," *Time*, November 29, 1994, pp. 52–59.

42. R. Ofshe and E. Watters, *Making Monsters*, p. 36.

43. R. Summit, "Memories true, otherwise" (Letters), *Psychiatric Times* 11 (1994): 16–17 (October); see also, M. J. Grinfeld, "International study finds no link between childhood sexual abuse and bulimia," *Psychi-*

atric Times 11 (1994): 8 (August), and "Impact of Ramona case uncertain," ibid. 11: 1, 3.

44. For example, see E. S. Blume, *Secret Survivors*; L. Terr, *Unchained Memories*; and note 56 in this chapter.

45. Advertisement, "True or false?" *New York Review of Books*, November 17, 1994, p. 3.

46. L. Terr, *Unchained Memories*.

47. D. Goleman, in note 39 in this chapter, emphasis added.

48. The Foundation, a tax-exempt institution, is located at 3508 Market Street, Suite 128, Philadelphia, PA 19104.

49. R. M. Dawes, *House of Cards*, p. 173.

50. See R. Summit, "Memories true, otherwise" (Letters), *Psychiatric Times* 11 (1994): 16–17. (October).

51. "Decalogue," *Encyclopaedia Britannica*, vol. 7, p. 153.

52. "Parents win suit against psychiatrist in sex case," *New York Times*, December 17, 1994, p. 9, emphasis added. Such reports are incredibly common nowadays. See also, D. Firestone, "Van drivers' charge of rape against officer called false," *New York Times*, December 16, 1994, pp. B1, B4.

53. "Parents win suit against psychiatrist in sex case," *New York Times*, December 17, 1994, p. 9.

54. M. J. Grinfeld, "Psychiatrist stung by huge damage award in repressed memory case," *Psychiatric Times* 12 (1995): 1, 22 (October), p. 1, emphasis added.

55. Ibid., p. 22.

56. For example, F. Crews, "The revenge of the repressed," *New York Review of Books*, November 17, 1994, pp. 54–60; "The Revenge of the repressed—Part II," ibid., December 1, 1994, pp. 49–58; "'Victims of memory': An exchange," ibid., January 12, 1995, pp. 42–48; and also M. Pendergast, *Victims of Memory*.

57. E. Bass and L. Davis, *The Courage to Heal*, p. 22.

58. Quoted in L. Jaroff, "Lies of the mind," *Time*, November 29, 1994, pp. 52–59.

59. L. Crook, "Repressed memory and rules of evidence," *New York Times Book Review*, March 26, 1995, p. 35; see also L. Terr, *Unchained Memories*, and R. Fredrickson, *Repressed Memories*.

60. Quoted in W. Goodman, "A growth industry: Helping recall sexual abuse," *New York Times*, April 4, 1995, p. C17.

61. Ibid.

62. E. Loftus and K. Ketcham, *The Myth of Repressed Memory*.

63. R. Ofshe, and E. Watters, *Making Monsters*, p. 44.

64. P. Cotton, "Biology enters repressed memory fray," *JAMA (Journal of the American Medical Association)* 272 (1994): 1725-1726. For the final report, see American Medical Association Council on Scientific

Affairs, "Report on memories of childhood sexual abuse," *International Journal of Clinical and Experimental Hypnosis* 43, pp. 114–117, 1995.

65. P. Cotton, note 64 in this chapter, p. 1725.

66. Ibid., p. 1726, emphasis added.

67. "Psychologists release statement about abuse memories," *Psychiatric News* 29 (1994): 4, emphasis added.

68. "Evaluating sex abuse 'memories,'" *New York Times*, November 15, 1994, p. C12.

69. Quoted in F. H. Frankel, "Discovering new memories in psychotherapy—childhood revisited, fantasy, or both?" *New England Journal of Medicine* 333 (1995): 591–594, p. 591; see also, American Psychiatric Association Board of Trustees, "Statement on memories of sexual abuse," *International Journal of Clinical and Experimental Hypnosis* 42 (1994): 261–264.

70. W. Reich, "The monsters in the mists," *New York Times Book Review*, May 15, 1994, pp. 1 ff; 38.

71. The Index to Freud's *Complete Psychological Works* lists three pages of double-columned entries for the word "repression;" see S. Freud, "Indexes," SE., vol. 24, pp. 364–367.

72. J. Breuer and S. Freud, *Studies on Hysteria* [1893–1895], in S. Freud, SE., vol. 2, p. 10, emphasis added.

73. S. Freud, "The Psychical Mechanism of Forgetfulness" [1898], in SE., vol. 3, p. 296, emphasis in the original.

74. S. Freud, "Screen Memories" [1899], in SE., vol. 3, p. 304, emphasis added.

75. U. Neisser, quoted in D. Goleman, "Studying the secrets of childhood memory: Researchers find recollection may be linked to language," *New York Times*, April 6, 1993, p. C1, C11.

76. Ibid.

77. S. Freud, "Construction in Analysis" [1937], in SE., vol. 23, p. 260.

78. S. Freud, "On the psychical mechanism of hysterical phenomena: A lecture" [1893], in SE., vol. 3, p. 38.

79. S. Freud, "The neuropsychoses of defence" [1894], SE., vol. 3, pp. 41–68; 48.

80. S. Freud, "Heredity and the aetiology of the neuroses" [1896], SE., vol. 3, pp. 152–153, emphasis added.

81. S. Freud, "Further remarks on the neuropsychoses of defence" [1896], SE., vol. 3, p. 164, emphasis added.

82. S. Freud, "Five lectures on psychoanalysis" [1909], SE., vol. 11, p. 16, emphasis in the original.

83. Ibid., p. 17.

84. J. Breuer and S. Freud, *Studies on Hysteria*, SE., vol. 2, p. 8, emphasis in the original.

85. Ibid., pp. 148–149.

86. S. Freud, "The psychogenesis of a case of homosexuality in a woman" [1920], SE., vol. 18, p. 160, emphasis in the original.

87. S. Freud, "An autobiographical study" [1925], SE., vol. 20, p. 63, emphasis added.

88. J. Breuer and S. Freud, Studies on Hysteria [1893–1895], in Freud, S., SE., vol. 2, pp. 148, 296.

89. S. Freud, "Further remarks on the neuropsychoses of defence" [1896], SE., vol. 3, p. 180.

90. For a sensitive, autobiographical portrayal of this theme with respect to the relations between the English and the Irish, see N. Browne, *Against the Tide*.

91. Romans 13:19. The Concordance to my Bible lists nineteen entries for Vengeance.

92. Matthew 9:6. This passage is repeated in Mark 2:10, and Luke 5:24.

93. A. Cohen, *Everyman's Talmud*, p. 65.

94. See I. Epstein, *Judaism*, especially pp. 175-176.

95. Leviticus 16:21.

96. Luke 23:34.

97. Daniel 9:9.

CHAPTER 4

1. B. Moyers, quoted in C. Dreifus, "Prince of PBS: Bill Moyers discusses mind/body healing," *Modern Maturity*, October-November, 1993, p. 68 ff; p. 70. The television series appeared in book form as B. Moyers, *Healing and the Mind*.

2. For a review of the vast literature on the neural basis of the mind, see D. M. Rosenthal, ed., *The Nature of Mind*.

3. A. J. Hobson, *The Chemistry of Conscious States*, pp. 6-7; and quoted from the review, J. Home, "Chemical engines of the soul," *Nature* 375 (1995): 459.

4. D. C. Dennett, *Consciousness Explained*, p. 33. See also, D. C. Dennett, "Our vegetative soul: The search for a reliable model of the human self," *TLS* (*Times Literary Supplement*, London), August 25, 1995, p. 3.

5. D. C. Dennett, *Darwin's Dangerous Idea*, quoted from the review, M. Ridley, "Here, there, everywhere," *Nature* 375 (1995): 457.

6. J. Cornwell, "Origin of the thesis," *The Sunday Times* (London), September 17, 1995, pp. 4–5.

7. J. M. Nash, A. Park, and J. Willwerth, "Glimpses of the mind," *Time*, July 17, 1995, pp. 44–52; p. 47.

8. D. C. Dennett, quoted in J. Cornwell, "Origin of the thesis," *The Sunday Times* (London), September 17, 1995, pp. 4–5; p. 5.

9. J. M. Nash, A. Park, and J. Willwerth, "Glimpses of the mind," *Time*, July 17, pp. 44–52.

10. Ibid.

11. P. M. Churchland, *The Engine of Reason, the Seat of the Soul*. For a generally sympathetic review, see R. Wright, "It's all in our heads," *New York Times Book Review*, July 9, 1995, pp. 1, 16–17.

12. Ibid, pp. 22–23, emphasis in the original.

13. Ibid., p. 181.

14. Ibid., p. 239.

15. Ibid., p. 269.

16. Ibid., p. 170.

17. Ibid., pp. 174, 176.

18. Ibid., p. 309.

19. Ibid., p. 311.

20. Ibid., pp. 313–314, emphasis added.

21. Ibid., pp. 312–313.

22. Ibid., p. 149.

23. Ibid., p. 319.

24. Ibid., p. 319, emphasis added.

25. A few people do. For a devastatingly critical review of Churchland's book, see J. Fodor, "West coast fuzzy: Why we don't know how the mind works," *TLS* (*Times Literary Supplement*, London), August 25, 1995, p. 5.

26. L. Baer, et al., "Automated telephone screening survey for depression," *JAMA* (*Journal of the American Medical Association*), 273 (1995): 1943–44.

27. H. Jackson, quoted in W. Penfield, "The Physiological Basis of the Mind," in S. M. Farber and R.H.L. Wilson, eds., *Control of the Mind*, pp. 12–13.

28. G. Steiner, *Real Presences*, p. 107.

29. J. R. Searle, quoted in T. Nagel, "The mind wins!" *New York Review of Books*, March 4, 1993, pp. 37–41; p. 40, emphasis added.

30. J. R. Searle, "The mystery of consciousness: Part I," *New York Review of Books*, November 2, 1995, pp. 60–66; p. 61; "Part II," ibid., November 16, 1995, pp. 54–61.

31. Ibid., pp. 60, 66.

32. Ibid., emphasis added.

33. Ibid., p. 62, emphasis added.

34. Ibid., p. 62, emphasis added.

35. J. R. Searle, *The Rediscovery of the Mind*, pp. xi, xii.

36. Ibid., p. 24, emphasis added.

37. Ibid., p. 227.

38. K. R. Popper and J. C. Eccles, *The Self and Its Brain*, p. 118.

39. Ibid., p. 118.

40. F. Crick, *The Astonishing Hypothesis*, pp. 3, 206, emphasis added. For a critical review, see J. C. Marshall, "The nerve cells of the soul," *New York Times Book Review*, January 16, 1994, p. 24.

41. Quoted in, J. C. Marshall, "The nerve cells of the soul," *New York Times Book Review*, January 16, 1994, p. 24.

42. Sir W. Lawrence, *Lectures on Physiology* (1819), quoted in A. Macalpine and R. Hunter, *Three Hundred Years of Psychiatry*, p. 749.

43. F. Crick, *The Astonishing Hypothesis*, pp. 187, 266.

44. Ibid., pp. 267–268.

45. J. Jaynes, *The Origin of Consciousness*, front and back of dust jacket.

46. Ibid., pp. 75, 405, emphasis in the original.

47. Ibid., p. 86, emphasis added.

48. See chapter 6; and, for example, P. K. McGuire et al., "Abnormal monitoring of inner speech: A physiological basis for auditory hallucinations," *The Lancet* 346 (1995): 596–600.

49. R. Restak, quoted in F. Crick, *The Astonishing Hypothesis*, back cover.

50. W. S. McCulloch, "The Past of a Delusion" (1953), in W. S. McCulloch, *Embodiments of Mind*, pp. 276–306; pp. 276–277.

51. D. Hofstadter, *Gödel, Escher, Bach*.

52. D. Hofstadter and the Fluid Analogies Research Group, *Fluid Concepts and Creative Analogies*, dust jacket and subtitle.

53. For example, see C. Lehmann-Haupt, "Can quantum mechanics explain consciousness?" *New York Times*, October 31, 1994, p. C20; J. Holt, "A lone scientist explains all human thought," *Wall Street Journal*, January 9, 1995, p. A12.

54. J. Holt, "A lone scientist explains all human thought," *Wall Street Journal*, January 9, 1995, p. A12.

55. R. Penrose, *Shadows of the Mind*, p. 28.

56. H. Putnam, "The best of all possible brains? A scientist speculates on what new sort of physics we would need to account for thought," *New York Review of Books*, November 20, 1994, p. 7.

57. J. Schwartz, "Brain v. computer: Penrose strikes again," *International Herald-Tribune*, December 9, 1994, p. 9.

58. R. Penrose, quoted in J. R. Searle, "The mystery of consciousness," *New York Review of Books*, November 2, 1995, pp. 60–66; p. 66.

59. J. Cornwell, "A mindfield for the brains trust," *Sunday Times* (London), September 4, 1994.

60. J. Gribbin, "The heaviness of being," *The Sunday Times Books* (London), December 18, 1994, p. 9.

61. For a respectful but skeptical review, see G. Johnson, "The odds on God," *New York Times Book Review*, October 9, 1994, pp. 15–16.

62. F. J. Tipler, *The Physics of Immortality*, p. ix.

63. Ibid., p. xi.

64. Ibid., p. 246.

65. Ibid., pp. 251, 253.

66. K. L. Woodward, "Angels," *Newsweek*, December 27, 1993, pp 52–57.

67. F. J. Tipler, op. cit., p. 220. Of course, not everyone is fooled. The reviewer in *Nature* dismisses *The Physics of Immortality* as "one of the most misleading books ever produced . . . a masterpiece of pseudo-science" (371: 115, September 8, 1994).

68. P. Davies and J. Gribbin, *The Matter Myth*, pp. 286, 308.

69. Quoted in "Physicist wins $1 million, links science, theology," *Syracuse Herald-Journal*, March 8, 1995, p. A6; and in G. Niebuhr, "Scientist wins religion prize of $1 million: Linking of theology and science is cited," *New York Times*, March 9, 1995, p. A13.

70. M. Gell-Mann, *The Quark and the Jaguar*, p. 21. The index to this book has no entry for "mind"; instead, it refers the reader to the entry for "brain and mind."

71. C. S. Lewis, *The Screwtape Letters*, p. 16.

72. I. Berlin, "Historical Inevitability" [1953], in I. Berlin, *Four Essays on Liberty*, pp. 116–117.

73. Many philosophers are also critical of reductionist approaches to the study of the mind. For example, see A. R. Louch, *Explanation and Human Action*; M. Peckham, *Explanation and Power*, and R. Abelson, *Lawless Minds* and *Persons*. Such writings receive virtually no mention in the popular press.

74. W. Heisenberg, *Physics and Philosophy*, pp. 106, 199.

75. M. Polanyi, *Personal Knowledge*, p. 335.

76. M. Polanyi, "Life's Irreducible Structures" [1968], in M. Polanyi, *Knowing and Being*, p. 238; see also W. Penfield, "The Physiological Basis of the Mind," in S. M. Farber and R.H.L. Wilson, eds., *Control of the Mind*, pp. 3–17.

77. J. McCrone, *The Myth of Irrationality*, p. 49.

78. Ibid., pp. 70, 230–231, 291.

79. Quoted in J. C. Marshall, "The nerve cells of the soul," *New York Times Book Review*, January 16, 1994, p. 24.

80. See chapter 2.

81. Chapter 2.

82. S. Begley, "One pill makes you larger, and one pill makes you small," *Newsweek*, February 7, 1994, pp. 37–40; p. 39.

83. B. Kantrowitz, "Computers as mind readers: In the future (maybe), your PC will be connected directly to your brain," *Newsweek*, May 30, 1994, p. 68.

84. J. M. Nash, A. Park, and J. Willwerth, "Glimpses of the mind," *Time*, July 17, 1995, pp. 44–52.

85. R. L. Gregory, ed., *The Oxford Companion to the Mind*, back page of dust jacket.

86. N. Malcolm, *Problems of Mind*, pp. 63–64, emphasis in the original.

87. D. A. Oakley and L. C. Eames, "The plurality of consciousness," in D. A. Oakley, ed., *Brain and Mind*, p. 236.

88. The entire November 1994 issue (volume 171) of the *Journal of Theoretical Biology* is devoted to this propaganda.

89. M. Merzenich, quoted in P. Cotton, "Neurophysiology, philosophy on collision course?" *JAMA* 269 (1993): 1485-86.

90. See chapter 2.

91. M. Merzenich, note 89 in this chapter, p. 1485.

92. Ibid., p. 1486.

93. See M. J. Grinfeld, "Ruling focuses on cause of mental illness," *Psychiatric Times* 11 (1994): 1, 7 (November), and "Insuror can't cut off benefits to bipolar patients, court rules," *Psychiatric News* 29 (1994): 1, 21 (November 11), citing: *Pat Roe v. Phoenix Home Life Mutual Life Insurance Company, et al.*, No. C 93–2894 WHO.

94. See M. J. Grinfeld, "Ruling focuses on cause of mental illness," *Psychiatric Times* 11 (1994): 1, 7 (November), p. 7, emphasis added.

95. See T. S. Szasz, *The Myth of Mental Illness* and *Insanity*.

96. A. J. Hobson, *The Chemistry of Conscious States*, p. 286.

97. D. Mash, quoted in F. Tasker, "The last frontier: Doctors who run endowment banks believe a brain, like a mind, is a terrible thing to waste," *Syracuse Herald-Journal*, April 1, 1994, pp. C1, C3.

98. Quoted in S. Blakeslee, "In brain's early growth, timetable may be crucial," *New York Times*, August 29, 1995, pp. C1, C3; p. C1.

99. S. Roan, "A poor state of mind," *Los Angeles Times*, September 19, 1995, pp. E1, E7; p. E7.

100. University of California, Los Angeles, "A free UCLA research study on the treatment of major depression in adolescents," flier, n.d. (1995).

101. Quoted in F. Tasker, "The last frontier: Doctors who run endowment banks believe a brain, like a mind, is a terrible thing to waste," *Syracuse Herald-Journal*, April 1, 1994, pp. C1, C3. See also note 30 in this chapter.

102. Quoted in M. R. Montgomery, "Picking brains: McLean organ bank may contain the key to curing many mental disorders," *Boston Globe*, February 12, 1994, pp. 61, 64.

103. J. B. Taylor, "Your brains needed for brain bank," *NAMI Advocate*, January-February 1994, p. 2.

104. Quoted in S. Chartrand, "Patents," *New York Times*, January 1, 1996, p. 46. The two subsequent quotations are from the same source.

105. W. F. Walsh, "Off the couch" (Letter), *The New York Times Magazine*, January 3, 1993, p. 6.

106. B. Moyers, *Healing and the Mind*, p. xiii.

107. R. Restak, *The Modular Brain*, p. 157.

CHAPTER 5

1. See G. Ryle, *The Concept of Mind*; M. Peckham, *Explanation and Power*; and C. M. Turbayne, *The Myth of Metaphor*.

2. J. Shafer, "Mind-Body Problem," in P. Edwards, ed., *The Encyclopedia of Philosophy*, vols. 5–6, pp. 336–346; p. 337.

3. B. Snell, *The Discovery of the Mind*, p. 6.

4. Ibid., p. 33.

5. See H. Jaffa, "Aristotle," in L. Strauss and J. Cropsey, eds., *History of Political Philosophy*, pp. 64–129; p. 65.

6. Ibid., p. 76, emphasis added.

7. G. Ryle, *The Concept of Mind*.

8. See chapter 2.

9. B. Williams, "Descartes, René," in P. Edwards, ed., *The Encyclopedia of Philosophy*, vols. 1–2, p. 344.

10. J. C. Traupman, *The New College Latin & English Dictionary*, p. 148. This dictionary does not list "mind" as one of the meanings of *ingenium*.

11. R. Descartes, *The Passions of the Soul*, in *The Philosophical Works of Descartes,* vol. 1, pp. 330 ff.

12. Ibid., p. 340.

13. Ibid., pp. 345, 347.

14. R. Descartes, *The Philosophical Writings of Descartes*, vol. 1, pp. 210, 280; and vol. 2, p. 109.

15. B. Williams, "Descartes, René," op. cit., p. 349.

16. Quoted in B. Stevenson, ed., *The Home Book of Quotations*, p. 1306. I assume that the original text uses the word "psyche."

17. John 1:1: ". . . and the Word was God." In this connection, see George Steiner's thought-provoking essay, *Real Presences*.

18. J. Bowker, *Problems of Suffering in Religions of the World*, p. 124.

19. A. MacIntyre, "Spinoza, Benedict (Baruch)," in P. Edwards, ed., *The Encyclopedia of Philosophy*, vols. 7–8, pp. 530–541; p. 531.

20. Quoted in J. P. Bradley et al., eds., *The International Dictionary of Thoughts*, p. 113.

21. Ibid.

22. F. J. Tipler, *The Physics of Immortality*, p. ix.

23. C. M. Turbayne, *The Myth of Metaphor*, p. 96.

24. I. Epstein, *Judaism*, p. 135.

25. M. Peckham, *Explanation and Power*, pp. 59–60.

26. Ibid., p. 2.

27. Ibid., p. 65, emphasis added.

28. Ibid.

29. A. Huxley, *Ends and Means*, p. 299.

30. C. Sagan, "Channeling and faith healing: Scam or miracle?" *Parade*, December 4, 1994, pp. 10–11; p. 11; the emphasis is Sagan's.

31. E. Ehrlich, *Amo, Amas, Amat, and More*, pp. 104–105.

32. W. Sargant, *The Battle for the Mind*.

33. J. Shafer, "Mind-Body Problem," note 2 in this chapter, p. 345.

34. Ibid.

35. For a typical example, see N. Humphrey, *A History of the Mind*.

36. See T. S. Szasz, *The Ethics of Psychoanalysis*, especially pp. 51–60.

37. See T. S. Szasz, *Anti-Freud*.

38. C. H. Whiteley, *Mind in Action*, p. 1.

39. Ibid., p. 2.

40. Ibid.

41. See especially C. W. Morris, "Introduction," in G. H. Mead, *Mind, Self, and Society*, pp. ix–xxxv.

42. Ibid., p. xxii.

43. G. H. Mead, *Mind, Self, and Society*, p. 191.

44. Ibid., p. 317.

CHAPTER 6

1. T. S. Szasz, *The Myth of Mental Illness* and *The Myth of Psychotherapy*.

2. Parts of this material have appeared in "Crazy talk: Thought disorder or psychiatric arrogance?" *British Journal of Medical Psychology* 66 (1993): 61–67. Reprinted by permission.

3. J. Leff, "Schizophrenia in the melting pot," *Nature* 353 (1991), 693–694.

4. T. S. Szasz, "Diagnoses are not diseases," *The Lancet*, 338 (1991): 1574–1576.

5. Sir M. Roth, "Schizophrenia and the theories of Thomas Szasz," *British Journal of Psychiatry*, 129 (1976): 317–326.

6. See, for example, R. E. Kendell, "The Classification and Phenomenology of Schizophrenia," in A. Kerr and P. Snaith, eds., *Contemporary Issues in Schizophrenia*, pp. 119–123. The index to this important volume has an entry for "thought disorders," p. 482.

7. E. Bleuler, *Dementia Praecox, oder Gruppe der Schizophrenien*.

8. E. Slater, and M. Roth, *Mayer-Gross Clinical Psychiatry*, pp. 266, 291, 316; emphasis added.

9. J. T. Marengo, M. Harrow, and W. S. Edell, "Thought Disorder," in C. G. Costello, ed., *Symptoms of Schizophrenia*, pp. 27–55; p. 27.

10. E. Bleuler, *Dementia Praecox*, p. 9.

11. Ibid., p. 123.

12. Ibid., p. 39.

13. Ibid., p. 150.

14. Ibid., p. 123.

15. *Cassell's German Dictionary*.

16. E. Bleuler, *Dementia Praecox*, p. 150.

17. Ibid., p. 438.

18. Ibid., pp. 488–489, emphasis added.

19. J. R. Smythies, "Wittgenstein's paranoia," *Nature* 350 (1991): 9, 1991.

20. M. Eliade, ed., *The Encyclopedia of Religion*, vol. 5, pp. 563–566.

21. *New Catholic Encyclopedia*, vol. 6, p. 473.

22. L. E. Hinsie and J. Shatzky, *Psychiatric Dictionary*.

23. J. M. Meth, "Exotic Psychiatric Syndromes," in S. Arieti and E. B. Brody, eds., *American Handbook of Psychiatry*, vol. 3, p. 728.

24. H. I. Kaplan and B. J. Sadock, "Typical Signs and Symptoms of Psychiatric Illness," in H. I. Kaplan and B. J. Sadock, eds., *Comprehensive Textbook of Psychiatry / V*, vol. 1, pp. 468–475; p. 472.

25. *New Encyclopaedia Britannica*, vol. 11, p. 842.

26. W. J. Samarin, *Tongues of Men and Angels*, p. xi.

27. Ibid., pp. 13–14.

28. "Poll: 7 percent of Americans have spoken in tongues," *Syracuse Herald-Journal*, October 28, 1995, p. A11.

29. See T. S. Szasz, ed., *The Age of Madness*.

30. See D. L. Rosenhan, "On being sane in insane places," *Science*, 179 (1993): 250–258. I remarked on this phenomenon in chapter 1.

31. See T. S. Szasz, *Schizophrenia*; and "Idleness and lawlessness in the Therapeutic State," *Society*, vol. 32, pp. 38–43 (May/June), 1995.

32. N. C. Andreasen, "Thought, language, and communication: II. Diagnostic significance," *Archives of General Psychiatry* 36 (1979): 1325–1330.

33. M. Harrow and M. Prosen, "Intermingling and disordered logic as influences on schizophrenic 'thought disorders,'" *Archives of General Psychiatry* 35 (1978): 1213–1218; and "Schizophrenic thought disorders: Bizarre associations and intermingling," *American Journal of Psychiatry* 36 (1979): 293–296; see also R. P. Bentall, H. F. Jackson, and D. Pilgrim, "Abandoning the concept of 'schizophrenia'": Some implications of validity arguments for psychological research into psychotic phenomena," *British Journal of Medical Psychology*, 27 (1988): 303–324; and "The concept of schizophrenia is dead: Long live the concept of schizophrenia?", *British Journal of Medical Psychology* 27 (1988): 329–331; and T. S. Szasz, *Schizophrenia*.

34. S. Rochester and J. R. Martin, *Crazy Talk*, pp. 2–3.

35. Ibid., p. 7.

36. See, generally, C. H. Brooks, *The Practice of Autosuggestion;* L. D. Weatherhead, *Psychology, Religion, and Healing,* pp. 122–128; and T. S. Szasz, *The Myth of Psychotherapy,* pp. 186–188.

37. G. R. Forrer, "Benign auditory and visual hallucinations," *Archives of General Psychiatry* 3 (1960): 119–122, p. 119; emphasis added.

38. T. B. Posey and M. E. Losch, "Auditory hallucinations of hearing voices in 375 normal subjects," *Imagination, Cognition, and Personality* 3 (1983–1984): 99–113

39. E. Bleuler, *Dementia Praecox,* p. 438.

40. S. Freud, *The Future of an Illusion* [1927], SE., vol. 21, p. 43.

41. Chapter 4.

42. J. Engel, quoted in D. Goleman, "Scientists trace 'voices' in schizophrenia," *New York Times,* September 22, 1993, p. C2, emphasis added.

43. P. K. McGuire, G. M. Shah, and R. M. Murray, "Increased blood flow in Broca's area during auditory hallucinations in schizophrenia," *The Lancet,* 342 (1993): 703–706, p. 706, emphasis added; see also J. L. Waddington, "Sight and insight: 'Visualisation' of auditory hallucinations in schizophrenia?," ibid., 342: 692–693 (September 18), 1993.

44. P. K. McGuire, et al., "Abnormal monitoring of inner speech: A physiological basis for auditory hallucinations," *The Lancet,* 346 (1995): 596–600, p. 600.

45. Ibid., p. 596.

46. J. Remvig, "Deaf-mutes with 'auditory' hallucinations," *Acta Psychiatrica Scandinavica* (Supplementum 206) 210 (1968): 111–120, p. 115; and G. R. Forrer, "Effect of oral activity on hallucinations," *AMA Archives of General Psychiatry* 2 (1960): 110–112.

47. American Psychiatric Association, *Diagnostic and Statistical Manual,* 3rd ed., p. 234.

48. H. I. Kaplan and B. J. Sadock, *Comprehensive Textbook of Modern Psychiatry / III,* p. 442.

49. J. A. Simons, D. B. Irwin, and B. A. Drinnin, *Psychology,* p. 526.

50. D. Henderson and I.R.C. Batchelor, *Henderson and Gillespie's Textbook of Psychiatry,* p. 163, emphasis added.

51. H. I. Kaplan and B. J. Sadock, note 48 in this chapter, p. 446.

52. E. Bleuler, *Dementia Praecox or the Group of Schizophrenias,* p. 150.

53. E. Slater and M. Roth, *Mayer-Gross Clinical Psychiatry,* pp. 275, 268.

54. E. Bleuler, note 52 in this chapter, pp. 148, 449. For the amazing story of two bright British girls, capable of speaking, who refused to speak to their parents and teachers, see M. Wallace, *The Silent Twins.*

55. Quoted in D. Grumbach, *Fifty Days of Solitude,* p. 64.

56. E. Bleuler, *Dementia Praecox,* p. 41.

57. H. I. Kaplan and B. J. Sadock, *Modern Synopsis of Comprehensive Textbook of Psychiatry/III*, 3rd ed., pp. 310–311.

58. T. S. Szasz, *Insanity*, pp. 237–278.

59. A. Clare, *Psychiatry in Dissent*, p. 87.

60. E. Bleuler, *Dementia Praecox or the Group of Schizophrenias*, pp. 97–98.

61. See, for example, J. Barron, "Woman pushed to her death in front of a subway," *New York Times*, January 5, 1995, pp. A1, B3; C. W. Dugger, "State called patient violent, then let him roam," ibid., January 7, 1995, pp. 1, 26; and B. Herbert, "Double-trouble killer," ibid., p. 23.

62. S. Kierkegaard, "A visit to the doctor" and "The diagnosis," in S. Kierkegaard, *Parables of Kierkegaard*, pp. 57, 95.

63. A. Bioy Casares, "Plans for an escape to Carmelo," *New York Review of Books*, April 10, 1986, p. 7.

64. J. Macmurray, *The Self as Agent* and *Persons in Relation*.

65. J. Macmurray, *The Self as Agent*, p. 98.

66. Ibid., pp. 173, 176, emphasis added.

67. J. Macmurray, *The Self as Agent*, p. 119.

68. J. Macmurray, *Persons in Relation*, p. 29.

69. A. Farrer, *The Freedom of the Will*, pp. 236–237.

70. Ibid., 237.

71. Many students of man have pointed out the epistemological incoherence of behaviorism. See, for example, A. Huxley, *Ends and Means*, p. 297.

72. J. B. Watson, "Psychology as a behaviorist views it," *Psychological Review*, 21 (1913): 158–177, p. 158; also in *Behaviorism* (University of Chicago Press, 1930), p. 6, emphasis in the original.

73. J. B. Watson, *Behaviorism* (Norton, 1924), pp. 233–234.

74. J. B. Watson, *Psychology From the Standpoint of a Behaviorist*, p. 420.

75. Ibid.

76. J. B. Watson, "Psychology as a behaviorist views it," *Psychological Review* 21 (1913): 158–177, p. 158, emphasis added.

77. J. B. Watson, *Behaviorism* (University of Chicago Press, 1930), pp. 297, 303.

78. Ibid., p. 303.

79. Ibid., p. 447.

80. Ibid., pp. 445–46, emphasis in the original.

81. B. F. Skinner, *Reflections on Behaviorism and Society*, p. 197.

82. B. F. Skinner, *Particulars of My Life*, p. 76, quoted in *Webster's II*, p. 218.

83. B. F. Skinner, *Science and Human Behavior*, p. 343.

84. B. F. Skinner, *About Behaviorism*, p. 103.

85. B. F. Skinner, *Upon Further Reflection*, p. 28.

86. R. D. Laing, *The Politics of Experience*; see also M. Barnes and J. Berke, *Mary Barnes*; R. Boyers, ed., *R. D. Laing and Anti-Psychiatry*; C. Sigal, *Zone of the Interior*; and A. Laing, *R. D. Laing*.

87. F. Basaglia, *Psychiatry Inside Out: Selected Writings of Franco Basaglia*.

88. See, generally, T. S. Szasz, *The Myth of Psychotherapy*; for specific examples, see S. Gilligan, and R. Price, *Therapeutic Conversations*, and D. Waters, "Prisoners of our metaphors: Do dialogic therapies make other methods obsolete?" *Family Therapy Networker* 18 (1994): 73–75.

89. W. H. Auden, *The Dyer's Hand*, p. 87.

EPILOGUE

1. G. S. Stent, "Molecular biology and metaphysics," *Nature* 248 (1974): 779–781.

2. S. Weinberg, "Reductionism redux," *New York Review of Books,* October 5, 1995, pp. 39–42; pp. 40–41, emphasis added.

3. Ibid., p. 40.

4. A. Camus, "The wager of our generation" [1957], in *Resistance, Rebellion, and Death*, p. 240.

5. J.-P. Sartre, *Being and Nothingness*, p. 554.

6. Ibid., p. 555.

7. See chapter 3.

8. J.-P. Sartre, *Being and Nothingness*, p. 51.

9. Ibid., p. 52, emphasis added. In his initial formulation of repression, Freud recognized the element of choice (see chapter 3).

10. M. Oakeshott, *Experience and Its Modes*, p. 1.

Bibliography

In addition to full reference to the books cited, the bibliography lists some of the other works consulted in the preparation of this work.

Abelson, R. *Lawless Minds*. Philadelphia: Temple University Press, 1988.

Abelson, R. *Persons: A Study in Philosophical Psychology*. New York: St. Martin's Press, 1977.

American Psychiatric Association. *Diagnostic and Statistical Manual of Mental Disorders*. 3rd ed. Washington, D. C.: American Psychiatric Association, 1980.

Andrade, E. N. de C. *Isaac Newton*. New York: Chanticleer Press, 1950.

Andreasen, N. C., ed. *Schizophrenia: From Mind to Molecule*. Washington, D.C.: American Psychiatric Association, 1994.

Andrews, R., ed. *The Columbia Dictionary of Quotations*. New York: Columbia University Press, 1993.

Arens, R. *Make Mad the Guilty: The Insanity Defense in the District of Columbia*. Springfield, IL: Charles C. Thomas, 1969.

Arieti, S. and E. B. Brody., eds. *American Handbook of Psychiatry*. 2nd ed. 3 vols. New York: Basic Books, 1974.

Aristotle. *The Basic Works of Aristotle*. Edited by Richard McKeon. New York: Random House, 1941.

Armstrong, D. M. *The Nature of Mind and Other Essays*. Ithaca, NY: Cornell University Press, 1981.

Armstrong, K. *A History of God: The 4000–Year Quest of Judaism, Christianity and Islam*. New York: Ballantine Books, 1993.

Auden, W. H. *The Dyer's Hand, and Other Essays* [1962]. New York: Vintage, 1968.

Bakhtin, M. M. *The Dialogic Imagination: Four Essays*. Translated by Caryl Emerson and Michael Holmquist. Austin: University of Texas Press, 1981.

Bakhtin, M. M. *Rabelais and His World*. Translated by Helene Iswolsky. Cambridge: MIT Press, 1968.

Bakhtin, M. M. *Speech Genres and Other Late Essays*. Translated by Vern W. McKee. Austin: University of Texas Press, 1986.

Bakhtin, M. M. *Toward a Philosophy of the Act*. Translated by Vadim Liapunov. Austin: University of Texas Press, 1993.

Bartlett's Familiar Quotations. 16th ed. Edited by Justin Kaplan. Boston: Little, Brown, 1992.

Basaglia, F. *Psychiatry Inside Out: Selected Writings of Franco Basaglia*. Edited by N. Schepper-Hughes, and A. M. Lovell. Translated by Anna M. Lovell and Teresa Shtob. New York: Columbia University Press, 1987.

Bass, E. and L. Davis. *The Courage to Heal: A Guide for Women Survivors of Child Sexual Abuse*. 3rd ed. New York: HarperCollins, 1994.

Batchelor, I.R.C. *Henderson and Gillespie's Textbook of Psychiatry*. 10th ed. London: Oxford University Press, 1969.

Beakley, B. and P. Ludlow, eds. *The Philosophy of Mind: Classical/Contemporary Issues*. Cambridge: MIT Press, 1992.

Beckman, P. *A History of PI*. Boulder: Golem Press, 1970.

Berlin, I. *Against the Current: Essays in the History of Ideas*. London: Hogarth Press, 1980.

Berlin, I. *Four Essays on Liberty*. London: Oxford University Press, 1969.

Bierce, A. *Poems of Ambrose Bierce*. Edited by M. E. Grenander. Lincoln, NE: University of Nebraska Press, 1995.

Black, H. C. *Black's Law Dictionary*. 4th ed. Revised. St. Paul: West Publishing Co., 1968.

Black, M. *The Labyrinth of Language*. New York: Mentor, 1969.

Blackstone, W. *Commentaries on the Laws of England: Of Public Wrongs* [1752–1765]. Boston: Beacon Press, 1962.

Bleuler, E. *Dementia Praecox oder Gruppe der Schizophrenien*. Leipzig: Franz Deuticke, 1911.

Bleuler, E. *Dementia Praecox or the Group of Schizophrenias* [1911]. Translated by Joseph Zinkin. New York: International Universities Press, 1950.

Blume, E. S. *Secret Survivors: Uncovering Incest and Its Aftermath in Women* [1990]. New York: Ballantine Books, 1993.

Bond, A. H. *Who Killed Virginia Woolf? A Psychobiography*. New York: Human Sciences Press, 1989.

Bowker, J. *Problems of Suffering in Religions of the World*. Cambridge: Cambridge University Press, 1970.

Bradley, J. P., L. F. Daniels, and T. C. Jones, eds. *The International Dictionary of Thoughts: An Encyclopedia of Quotations from Every Age for Every Occasion*. Chicago: J. G. Ferguson Publishing Co., 1969.

Bremmer, J. and H. Roodenburg, eds. *A Cultural History of Gesture*. Ithaca: Cornell University Press, 1992.

Brooks, C. H. *The Practice of Autosuggestion by the Method of Émile Coué*. Revised with a foreword by Émile Coué. New York: Dodd, Mead, 1922.

Browne, N. *Against the Tide*. Dublin: Gill and Macmillan, 1986.

Bruce, R. V. *Bell: Alexander Graham Bell and the Conquest of Solitude*. Boston: Little Brown, 1973.

Burnham, S. *A Book of Angels*. New York: Ballantine Books, 1991.

Butler, J. *Butler's Fifteen Sermons, Preached at the Rolls Chapel and a Dissertation on the Nature of Virtue* [1726, 1736]. Edited by T. A. Roberts. London: Society for the Promotion of Christian Knowledge, 1970.

Camus, A. *Resistance, Rebellion, and Death*. Translated by Justin O'Brien. New York: Knopf, 1961.

Carroll, J. B. *Language and Thought*. Englewood Cliffs, NJ: Prentice Hall, 1964.

Carroll, L. *Alice's Adventures in Wonderland* [1865]; and *Through the Looking-Glass, and What Alice Found There* [1871]. M. Gardner, ed. *The Annotated Alice*. Harmondsworth: Penguin, 1960.

Cassell's German Dictionary, The New. Edited by Harold T. Betteridge. New York: Funk & Wagnalls, 1958.

Cavalieri, P. and P. Singer, eds. *The Great Ape Project: Equality Beyond Humanity*. New York: St. Martin's Press, 1993.

Chesterton, G. K. *Orthodoxy*. London: John Lane, 1909.

Chomsky, N. *Cartesian Linguistics*. New York: Harper & Row, 1966.

Chomsky, N. *Language and Mind*. Enlarged edition. New York: Harcourt Brace, 1972.

Churchland, P. M. *The Engine of Reason, the Seat of the Soul: A Philosophical Journey Into the Brain*. Cambridge: MIT Press, 1995.

Churchland, P. M. *Matter and Consciousness*. Cambridge: MIT Press, 1988.

Churchland, P. S. *Neurophilosophy: Toward a Unified Science of the Mind-Brain*. Cambridge: MIT Press, 1986.

Churchland, P. S. and T. S. Sejnowski. *The Computational Brain*. Cambridge: MIT Press, 1992.

Clare, A. *Psychiatry in Dissent*. London: Tavistock, 1976.

Cohen, A. *Everyman's Talmud*. New York: Schocken Books, 1975.

Cohen, L. H. *Train Go Sorry: Inside a Deaf World*. Boston: Houghton Mifflin, 1994.

Cooper, D., ed. *The Dialectics of Liberation*. Harmondsworth: Penguin, 1968.

Corsini, R. J., ed. *Encyclopedia of Psychology*. 4 vols. New York: Wiley, 1984.

Costello, C. G., ed. *Symptoms of Schizophrenia*. New York: Wiley, 1993.

Crick, F. *The Astonishing Hypothesis: The Scientific Search for the Soul*. New York: Charles Scribner's Sons, 1994.

Damasio, A. R. *Descartes' Error: Emotion, Reason, and the Human Brain*. New York: Putnam, 1994.

Davies, P. *Are We Alone? Philosophical Implications of the Discovery of Extraterrestrial Life*. New York: Basic Books, 1995.

Davies, P. *The Mind of God: The Scientific Basis for a Rational World*. New York: Simon and Schuster, 1992.

Davies, P. and J. Gribbin. *The Matter Myth: Dramatic Discoveries That Challenge Our Understanding of Physical Reality*. New York: Simon and Schuster, 1992.

Dawes, R. *House of Cards: The Collapse of Modern Psychotherapy*. New York: Free Press, 1993.

Dennett, D. C. *Consciousness Explained*. Boston: Little, Brown & Co., 1991.

Dennett, D. C. *Darwin's Dangerous Idea: Evolution and the Meanings of Life*. New York: Simon and Schuster, 1995.

Dennett, D. C. *The Intentional Stance*. Cambridge: MIT Press, 1987.

Descartes, R. *The Philosophical Works of Descartes*. Translated by Elisabeth S. Haldane and G.R.T. Ross. 2 vols. Cambridge: The University Press, 1968.

Descartes, R. *The Philosophical Writings of Descartes*. Translated by John Cottingham, Robert Stoothoff, and Douglas Murdoch. 3 vols. Cambridge: Cambridge University Press, 1985.

Eddy, M. B. *Science and Health, with Key to the Scriptures* [1875]. Boston: The First Church of Christ, 1971.

Edelman, G. M. *Bright Air, Brilliant Fire: On the Matter of the Mind*. New York: Basic Books, 1992.

Edelman, G. M. *The Remembered Present: A Biological Theory of Consciousness*. New York: Basic Books, 1995.

Edwards, J. *Freedom of the Will* [1754]. Edited by Arnold S. Kaufman and William K. Frankena. Indianapolis: Bobbs-Merrill, 1969.

Edwards, P., ed. *The Encyclopedia of Philosophy*. 8 vols. New York: Collier Macmillan, 1967.

Ehrlich, E. *Amo, Amas, Amat and More: How to Use Latin to Your Own Advantage and to the Astonishment of Others*. New York: Harper & Row, 1985.

Eliade, M., ed. *The Encyclopedia of Religion*. New York: Macmillan, 1987.

Encyclopedia of Philosophy, The. Edited by Paul Edwards. 8 vols. New York: Collier Macmillan, 1967.

Epstein, I. *Judaism: A Historical Interpretation*. New York: Penguin, 1982.

Farber, S. M. and R.H.L. Wilson, eds. *Control of the Mind: A Symposium.* New York: McGraw-Hill, 1961.

Farrer, A. *The Freedom of the Will.* London: Adam & Charles Black, 1958.

Feinberg, J., ed. *Moral Concepts.* London: Oxford University Press, 1969.

Finkelhorn, D. *Child Sexual Abuse: New Theory and Research.* New York: Free Press, 1984.

Fredrickson, R. *Repressed Memories: A Journey to Recovery from Sexual Abuse.* New York: Fireside/Simon and Schuster, 1992.

Freeman, E. E. *Angelic Healing: Working with Your Angels to Heal Your Life.* New York: Warner Books, 1994.

Freeman, L. *The Story of Anna O.* New York: Walker and Company, 1972.

Freud, S. *The Standard Edition of the Complete Psychological Works of Sigmund Freud.* Translated by James Strachey. 24 vols. London: Hogarth Press, 1953–1974. (Cited as SE.)

Furth, H. G. *Thinking Without Language: Psychological Implications of Deafness.* New York: Free Press, 1966.

Gell-Mann, M. *The Quark and the Jaguar: Ventures in the Simple and the Complex.* New York: W. H. Freeman, 1995.

Gilligan, S. and R. Price. *Therapeutic Conversations.* New York: Norton, 1993.

Gleick, J. *Genius: The Life and Science of Richard Feynman.* New York: Pantheon, 1992.

Goswami, A. *The Self-Aware Universe: How Consciousness Creates the Material World.* New York: Tarcher/Putnam, 1993.

Gottschalk, L. A. and G. C. Gleser. *The Measurement of Psychological States Through the Content Analysis of Verbal Behavior.* Berkeley: University of California Press, 1969.

Gregory, R. L., ed. *The Oxford Companion to the Mind.* New York: Oxford University Press, 1987.

Griffin, D. R. *Animal Minds.* Chicago: University of Chicago Press, 1992.

Gross, D., ed. *Dictionary of the Jewish Religion.* New York: Bantam Books, 1979.

Grumbach, D. *Fifty Days of Solitude.* Boston: Beacon Press, 1994.

Harre, R. and G. Gillett. *The Discursive Mind.* Thousand Oaks, CA: Sage Publications, 1994.

Hauck, R., ed. *Angels: The Mysterious Messengers.* New York: Ballantine Books, 1994.

Hayek, F. A. *The Constitution of Liberty.* Chicago: University of Chicago Press, 1960.

Hayek, F. A. *The Counter-Revolution of Science: Studies on the Abuse of Reason* [1955]. New York: Free Press, 1964.

Hearne, V. *Animal Happiness.* New York: HarperCollins, 1994.

Heisenberg, W. *Physics and Philosophy: The Revolution in Modern Science*. New York: Harper & Row, 1958.

Henderson, D. and I.R.C. Batchelor. *Henderson and Gillespie's Textbook of Psychiatry*. London: Oxford University Press, 1962.

Hilts, P. J. *Memory's Ghost: The Strange Tale of Mr. M and the Nature of Memory*. New York: Simon and Schuster, 1995.

Hinsie, L. E. and J. Shatzky. *Psychiatric Dictionary*. New York: Oxford University Press, 1953.

Hobson, J. A. *The Chemistry of Conscious States: How The Brain Changes Its Mind*. Boston: Little, Brown, 1994.

Hofstadter, D. *Gödel, Escher, Bach: An Eternal Golden Braid*. New York: Basic Books, 1979.

Hofstadter, D. and the Fluid Analogies Research Group. *Fluid Concepts and Creative Analogies: Computer Models of the Fundamental Mechanisms of Thought*. New York: Basic Books, 1995.

The Holy Bible, Authorized King James Version. Glasgow: R. L. Allan & Son, 1931.

Humphrey, N. *Consciousness Regained*. New York: Oxford University Press, 1983.

Humphrey, N. *A History of the Mind*. New York: Simon and Schuster, 1992.

Huxley, A. *Ends and Means: An Inquiry into the Nature of Ideals and into the Methods Employed for Their Realization* [1937]. New York: Greenwood Press, 1969.

Isaacson, B. *Dictionary of the Jewish Religion*. New York: Bantam Books, 1979.

Jackendoff, R. *Patterns in the Mind: Language and Human Nature*. New York: Basic Books, 1994.

Jaki, S. L. *Brain, Mind, and Computers* [1969]. Washington, D.C.: Regnery Gateway, 1989.

Jaynes, J. *The Origin of Consciousness in the Breakdown of the Bicameral Mind*. Boston: Houghton Mifflin, 1977.

Johnson, F. H. *The Anatomy of Hallucinations*. Chicago: Nelson-Hall, 1978.

Josipovici, G. *The Book of God: A Response to the Bible*. New Haven: Yale University Press, 1988.

Kafka, F. *The Penal Colony: Stories and Short Pieces*. Translated by Willa and Edwin Muir. New York: Schocken, 1948.

Kant, I. *Kant: Werke in 12 Bänden*. Edited by Wilhelm Weischedel. Frankfurt: Insel Verlag, 1964.

Kaplan, H. I. and B. J. Sadock. *Comprehensive Textbook of Psychiatry/V*. 5th ed. 2 vols. Baltimore: Williams & Wilkins, 1985.

Kaplan, H. I. and B. J. Sadock. *Modern Synopsis of Comprehensive Textbook of Psychiatry/III*. 3rd ed. Baltimore: Williams & Wilkins, 1982.

Keller, H. *The Story of My Life* [1902]. New York: Dell, 1961.

Kerr, A. and P. Snaith, eds. *Contemporary Issues in Schizophrenia*. London: Gaskell/Royal College of Psychiatrists, 1986.

Kierkegaard, S. *Parables of Kierkegaard*. Edited by Thomas C. Ogden. Princeton: Princeton University Press, 1978.

Kleinig, J. *Paternalism*. Totowa, NJ: Rowman and Allanheld, 1984.

Kolb, L. C. *Noyes' Modern Clinical Psychiatry*. 7th ed. Philadelphia: Saunders, 1968.

Kotre, J. *White Gloves: How We Create Ourselves Through Memory*. New York: Free Press, 1995.

Kraepelin, E. *Psychiatry: A Textbook for Students and Physicians*. [1899]. Translated by Jacques M. Quen. Canton, MA: Science History Publications, 1990.

Kyle, G. J. and B. Woll. *Sign Language: The Study of Deaf People and Their Language*. Cambridge: Cambridge University Press, 1985.

Laing, R. D. *The Politics of Experience and the Bird of Paradise*. Harmondsworth: Penguin, 1967.

Laird, C. *The Miracle of Language* [1953]. New York: Fawcett, 1957.

Lane, H. *When the Mind Hears: A History of the Deaf*. New York: Random House, 1984.

Lane, H. *The Wild Boy of Aveyron*. Cambridge: Harvard University Press, 1976.

Langer, S. K. *Mind: An Essay on Human Feeling*. 3 vols. Johns Hopkins University Press, 1967.

Langer, S. K. *Philosophical Sketches: A Study of the Human Mind in Relation to Feeling, Explored Through Art, Language, and Symbol* [1962]. New York: Mentor, 1964.

Langer, S. K. *Philosophy in a New Key: A Study in the Symbolism of Reason, Rite, and Art* [1942]. New York: Mentor, 1956.

Lenard, P. *Great Men of Science: A History of Scientific Progress* [1933]. Translated by H. Stafford Hatfield. New York: Macmillan, 1935.

Lewis, C. S. *The Business of Heaven: Daily Readings from C. S. Lewis*. Edited by Walter Hooper. New York: Harcourt Brace Jovanovich, 1984.

Lewis, C. S. *The Screwtape Letters & Screwtape Proposes a Toast* [1959]. New York: Macmillan, 1967.

Loftus, E. and K. Ketcham. *The Myth of Repressed Memory: False Memories and Allegations of Sexual Abuse*. New York: St. Martin's Press, 1994.

Louch, A. R. *Explanation and Human Action*. Berkeley: University of California Press, 1988.

Macalpine, I. and R. Hunter. *Three Hundred Years of Psychiatry, 1535–1860: A History Presented in Selected English Texts*. New York: Oxford University Press, 1963.

Mack, J. E. *Abduction: Human Encounters with Aliens*. New York: Macmillan, 1994.

Mackay, C. *Extraordinary Popular Delusions and the Madness of Crowds* [1841, 1852]. New York: Noonday Press, 1962.

Macmurray, J. *Persons in Relation*. London: Faber and Faber, 1961.

Macmurray, J. *The Self as Agent* [1957]. London: Faber and Faber, 1969.

Macpherson, C. B. *The Political Theory of Possessive Individualism: Hobbes to Locke*. London: Oxford University Press, 1962.

Malcolm, N. *Problems of Mind: Descartes to Wittgenstein*. New York: Harper & Row, 1971.

Mann, D. W. *A Simple Theory of the Self*. New York: Norton, 1994.

Maritain, J. *Moral Philosophy: An Historical and Critical Survey of the Great Systems* [1960]. New York: Charles Scribner's Sons, 1964.

Martin, R. *Out of Silence: A Journey Into Language*. New York: Henry Holt, 1994.

McClure, G. W. *Sorrow and Consolation in Italian Humanism*. Princeton: Princeton University Press, 1991.

McCrone, J. *The Myth of Irrationality: The Science of the Mind from Plato to "Star Trek."* London: Macmillan, 1993.

McCulloch, W. S. *Embodiments of Mind*. Cambridge: MIT Press, 1965.

McDannell, C. and B. Lang. *Heaven: A History*. New Haven: Yale University Press, 1988.

McWilliams, P. *Ain't Nobody's Business If You Do: The Absurdity of Consensual Crimes in a Free Society*. Los Angeles: Prelude Press, 1993.

Mead, G. H. *Mind, Self & Society: From the Standpoint of a Social Behaviorist*. Edited by Charles W. Morris. Chicago: University of Chicago Press, 1934.

Mead, G. H. *The Philosophy of the Present* [1932]. Edited by Arthur E. Murphy. Chicago: University of Chicago Press, 1980.

Mead, G. H. *Philosophy, Social Theory, and the Thought of George Herbert Mead*. Edited by Mitchell Aboulafia. New York: State University of New York Press, 1991.

Miles, J. *God: A Biography*. New York: Knopf, 1995.

Milgram, S. *Obedience to Authority: An Experimental View*. New York: Harper & Row, 1969.

Miller, R. B. *The Restoration of Dialogue: Readings in the Philosophy of Psychology*. Washington, D.C.: American Psychological Association, 1992.

Minsky, M. *The Society of Mind*. New York: Simon and Schuster, 1986.

Mitchell, R. *Less Than Words Can Say*. Boston: Little, Brown, 1979.

Montaigne, M. de. *Essays* [1580]. Translated by J. M. Cohen. Baltimore: Penguin, 1958.

Morgan, G. C. *The Voice of the Devil*. New York: Fleming H. Revell, n.d.

Morris, C. *The Discovery of the Individual, 1050–1200*. New York: Harper & Row, 1972.

Morris, C. S. *Six Theories of Mind*. Chicago: University of Chicago Press, 1932.

Moyers, B. *Healing and the Mind*. New York: Doubleday, 1993.

Müller, F. M. *The Science of Thought* [1887]. Reprint of the 1887 edition, published by Longmans, Green, and Co., London; New York: AMS Press, 1987.

Murray, G. *Five Stages of Greek Religion* [1912/1951]. Garden City, NY: Doubleday Anchor, 1955.

Neisser, U. and E. Winograd, eds. *Remembering Reconsidered: Ecological and Traditional Approaches to the Study of Memory*. Cambridge: University Press, 1988.

New Catholic Encyclopedia. Washington, D.C.: Catholic University of America, 1967.

New Encyclopaedia Britannica. Chicago: Encyclopaedia Britannica, 1990.

Noël, L. *Intolerance: A General Survey*. Translated by Arnold Bennett. Montreal and Kingston: McGill-Queen's University Press, 1994.

Nussbaum, M. C. *The Therapy of Desire: Theory and Practice in Hellenistic Ethics*. Princeton: Princeton University Press, 1994.

Oakeshott, M. *Experience and Its Modes* [1933]. New York: Cambridge University Press, 1985.

Oakeshott, M. *On Human Conduct*. Oxford: Clarendon Press, 1975.

Oakley, D. A., ed. *Brain and Mind*. London: Methuen, 1985.

Ofshe, R. and E. Watters. *Making Monsters: False Memories, Psychotherapy, and Sexual Hysteria*. New York: Scribner's, 1994.

Orieux, J. *Voltaire*. Translated by Barbara Bray and Helen R. Lane. Garden City, NY: Doubleday, 1979.

Paine, A. B. *Mark Twain: A Biography*. 3 vols. New York: Harper & Brothers, 1912.

Peckham, M. *Explanation and Power: The Control of Human Behavior*. New York: Seabury Press/Continuum, 1979.

Peirce, C. S. *Values in a Universe of Chance: Selected Writings of Charles S. Peirce (1839–1914)*. Edited by Philip P. Wiener. Garden City, NY: Doubleday Anchor, 1958.

Pendergast, M. *Victims of Memory: Incest Accusations and Shattered Lives*. Hinesburg, VT: Upper Access, 1995.

Penfield, W. and L. Roberts. *Speech and Brain-Mechanisms*. Princeton: Princeton University Press, 1959.

Penrose, R. *The Emperor's New Mind: Concerning Computers, Minds, and the Laws of Physics*. New York: Oxford University Press, 1989.

Penrose, R. *Shadows of the Mind: A Search for the Missing Science of Consciousness*. New York: Oxford University Press, 1994.

Phillips, D. B., ed. *The Choice Is Always Ours: An Anthology on the Religious Way*. Rindge, NH: Richard R. Smith, 1954.

Pinker, S. *The Language Instinct*. New York: William Morrow, 1994.

Plato. *The Collected Dialogues of Plato, Including the Letters*. Edited by Edith Hamilton and Huntington Cairns. Princeton: Princeton University Press, 1973.

Polanyi, M. *Knowing and Being: Essays by Michael Polanyi*. Edited by Marjorie Greene. Chicago: University of Chicago Press, 1968.

Polanyi, M. *Personal Knowledge: Towards a Post-Critical Philosophy*. Chicago: University of Chicago Press, 1958.

Polkinghorne, J. *The Faith of a Physicist: Reflections of a Bottom-Up Thinker*. Princeton: Princeton University Press, 1994.

Popper, K. R. and J. C. Eccles. *The Self and Its Brain*. New York: Springer International, 1977.

Restak, R. *The Modular Brain: How New Discoveries in Neuroscience Are Answering Age-Old Questions About Memory, Free Will, Consciousness, and Personal Identity*. New York: Simon and Schuster, 1995.

Rochester, S. and J. R. Martin. *Crazy Talk: A Study of the Discourse of Schizophrenic Speakers*. New York: Plenum Press, 1979.

Rorty, R. *Philosophy and the Mirror of Nature*. Princeton: Princeton University Press, 1979.

Rosenfield, I. *The Strange, Familiar, and Forgotten: An Anatomy of Consciousness*. New York: Vintage, 1995.

Rosenhan, D. L. and M.E.P. Seligman. *Abnormal Psychology*. New York: Norton, 1984.

Rosenthal, D. M., ed. *The Nature of Mind*. New York: Oxford University Press, 1991.

Ruesch, J. *Therapeutic Communication*. New York: Norton, 1961.

Ruesch, J. and G. Bateson. *Communication: The Social Matrix of Psychiatry*. New York: Norton, 1951.

Rychlak, J. E. *Discovering Free Will and Personal Responsibility*. New York: Oxford University Press, 1979.

Ryle, G. *The Concept of Mind*. London: Hutchinson's University Library, 1949.

Samarin, W. J. *Tongues of Men and Angels: The Religious Language of Pentecostalism*. New York: Macmillan, 1972.

Sargant, W. *Battle for the Mind: A Physiology of Conversion and Brainwashing* [1957]. New York: Harper & Row, 1971.

Sartorius, R., ed. *Paternalism*. Minneapolis: University of Minnesota Press, 1983.

Sartre, J.-P. *Being and Nothingness: An Essay on Phenomenological Ontology*. Translated by H. Barnes. New York: Philosophical Library, 1956.

Sartre, J.-P. *Sketch for a Theory of the Emotions* [1939]. Translated by Philip Mairet. London: Methuen, 1962.

Sartre, J.-P. *The Words*. Translated by Bernard Frechtman. New York: Braziller, 1964.

Schlesinger, I. M. and L. Namir, eds. *Sign Language of the Deaf: Psychological, Linguistic, and Sociological Perspectives*. New York: Academic Press, 1978.

Schoeck, H. and J. W. Wiggins, eds. *Psychiatry and Responsibility*. Princeton: Van Nostrand, 1962.

Schrodinger, E. *What Is Life? The Physical Aspects of the Living Cell*. New York: Macmillan, 1946.

Screech, M. A. *Montaigne and Melancholy: The Wisdom of the Essays*. London: Penguin, 1991.

Searle, J. R. *The Rediscovery of the Mind*. Cambridge: MIT Press, 1992.

Sigal, C. *Zone of the Interior*. New York: Popular Library, 1978.

Simons, J. A., D. B. Irwin, and B. A. Drinnin. *Psychology: The Search for Understanding*. St. Paul: West Publishing Co., 1987.

Skinner, B. F. *About Behaviorism*. New York: Knopf, 1974.

Skinner, B. F. *Reflections on Behaviorism and Society*. Englewood Cliffs, NJ: Prentice Hall, 1978.

Skinner, B. F. *Science and Human Behavior*. New York: Free Press, 1953.

Skinner, B. F. *Upon Further Reflection*. Englewood Cliffs, NJ: Prentice Hall, 1987.

Slade, P. D. and R. P. Bentall. *Sensory Deception: A Scientific Analysis of Hallucination*. Baltimore: Johns Hopkins University Press, 1988.

Slater, E. and M. Roth. *Mayer-Gross Clinical Psychiatry*. 3rd ed. Baltimore: Williams and Wilkins, 1969.

Slovenko, R. *Psychiatry and Criminal Culpability*. New York: Wiley, 1995.

Snell, B. *The Discovery of the Mind: The Greek Origins of European Thought* [1948]. Translated by T. G. Rosenmeyer. New York: Harper Torchbook, 1960.

Sokolov, A. N. *Inner Speech and Thought* [1968]. Translated by George T. Onischenko. New York: Plenum Press, 1972.

Sperry, R. *Science and Moral Priority: Merging Mind, Brain, and Human Values*. New York: Columbia University Press, 1983.

Spicker, S. F., ed. *The Philosophy of the Body: Rejections of Cartesian Dualism*. New York: Quadrangle, 1970.

Sprott, S. E. *The English Debate on Suicide: From Donne to Hume*. LaSalle, IL: Open Court, 1961.

Stangerup, H. *The Man Who Wanted to Be Guilty* [1982]. Translated by David Gres-Wright. London: Marion Boyars, 1991.

Steiner, G. *Real Presences*. Chicago: University of Chicago Press, 1989.

Stent, S. G., ed. *Morality as a Biological Phenomenon: The Presuppositions of Sociobiological Research*. Berkeley: University of California Press, 1980.

Stevenson, B., ed. *The Home Book of Quotations, Classical and Modern*. New York: Dodd, Mead, 1958.

Stevenson, B., ed. *The Macmillan Book of Proverbs, Maxims, and Famous Phrases*. New York: Macmillan, 1948.

Stokoe, W. C., Jr. *Semiotics and Human Sign Languages*. The Hague: Mouton, 1972.

Storr, A. *Solitude: A Return to the Self*. New York: Free Press, 1988.

Strauss, L. and J. Cropsey, eds. *History of Political Philosophy*. 2nd ed. Chicago: Rand McNally, 1972.

Strauss, M. B., ed. *Familiar Medical Quotations*. Boston: Little, Brown, 1968.

Strawson, G. *Mental Reality*. Cambridge: MIT Press, 1994.

Szasz, T. S. *Anti-Freud: Karl Kraus's Criticism of Psychoanalysis and Psychiatry* [1976]. Syracuse: Syracuse University Press, 1990.

Szasz, T. S. *Ceremonial Chemistry: The Ritual Persecution of Drugs, Addicts, and Pushers*. Garden City, NY: Doubleday/Anchor, 1974.

Szasz, T. S. *Cruel Compassion: Psychiatric Control of Society's Unwanted*. New York: Wiley, 1994.

Szasz, T. S. *The Ethics of Psychoanalysis: The Theory and Method of Autonomous Psychotherapy* [1965]. Syracuse: Syracuse University Press, 1988.

Szasz, T. S. *Insanity: The Idea and Its Consequences*. New York: Wiley, 1987.

Szasz, T. S. *A Lexicon of Lunacy: Metaphoric Malady, Moral Responsibility, and Psychiatry*. Brunswick, NJ: Transaction, 1993.

Szasz, T. S. *The Manufacture of Madness: A Comparative Study of the Inquisition and the Mental Health Movement*. New York: Harper & Row, 1970.

Szasz, T. S. *The Myth of Mental Illness: Foundations of a Theory of Personal Conduct*. New York: Hoeber-Harper, 1961; revised ed. New York: Harper & Row, 1974.

Szasz, T. S. *The Myth of Psychotherapy: Mental Healing as Religion, Repression, and Rhetoric* [1978]. Syracuse: Syracuse University Press, 1988.

Szasz, T. S. *Our Right to Drugs: The Case for a Free Market*. New York: Praeger, 1992; Syracuse: Syracuse University Press, 1996.

Szasz, T. S. *Schizophrenia: The Sacred Symbol of Psychiatry* [1976]. Syracuse: Syracuse University Press, 1988.

Szasz, T. S. *The Second Sin*. Garden City, NY: Doubleday/Anchor, 1973.

Szasz, T. S. *Sex By Prescription* [1980]. Syracuse: Syracuse University Press, 1990.

Szasz, T. S. *The Therapeutic State: Psychiatry in the Mirror of Current Events*. Buffalo: Prometheus Books, 1984.

Szasz, T. S. *The Untamed Tongue*. LaSalle, IL: Open Court, 1990.

Szasz, T. S., ed. *The Age of Madness: A History of Involuntary Mental Hospitalization Presented in Selected Texts*. Garden City, NY: Doubleday/Anchor, 1973.

Talmud, The Living: The Wisdom of the Fathers. Selected and translated by Judah Goldin. New York: Mentor, 1957.

Terr, L. *Unchained Memories: True Stories of Traumatic Memories, Lost and Found*. New York: Basic Books, 1994.

Thaddeus, V. *Voltaire: Genius of Mockery*. New York: Brentano's, 1928.

Tipler, F. J. *The Physics of Immortality: Modern Cosmology, God, and the Resurrection of the Dead*. New York: Doubleday, 1994.

Traupman, J. C. *The New College Latin & English Dictionary*. New York: Bantam, 1966.

Turbayne, C. M. *The Myth of Metaphor*. Revised ed. Columbia, SC: University of South Carolina Press, 1970.

Twain, M. *The Mammoth Cod, an Address to the Stomach Club*. Introduction by G. Legman. Waukesha, WI: Maledicta Press, 1976.

Vigotsky, L. *Thought and Language* [1934]. Translated by Alex Kozulin. Cambridge, MA: MIT Press, 1993.

Vlastos, G. *Socrates: Ironist and Moral Philosopher*. Ithaca, NY: Cornell University Press, 1991.

Wallace, M. *The Silent Twins*. New York: Prentice-Hall, 1986.

Watson, J. B. *Behavior: An Introduction to Comparative Psychology*. New York: Holt, 1914.

Watson, J. B. *Behaviorism*. New York: Norton, 1924.

Watson, J. B. *Behaviorism*. Chicago: University of Chicago Press, 1930.

Watson, J. B. *Psychology from the Standpoint of a Behaviorist*. Philadelphia: Lippincott, 1919.

Weatherhead, L. D. *Psychology, Religion, and Healing*. Revised ed. New York: Abingdon Press, 1952.

Webster's II, New Riverside Desk Quotations. Edited by James B. Simpson. Boston: Houghton Mifflin, 1992.

Webster's Third New International Dictionary. Springfield, MA: G. & C. Merriam Co., 1961.

Weiskrantz, L., ed. *Thought Without Language*. Oxford: Clarendon Press, 1988.

Wells, G. A. *What's In a Name? Reflections on Language, Magic, and Religion*. Chicago: Open Court, 1993.

Werblowsly, R. J. and J. Wigoder, eds. *The Encyclopedia of the Jewish Religion*. New York: Holt, Rinehart and Winston, 1965.

Wertsch, J. V. *Vigotsky and the Social Formation of Mind*. Cambridge: Harvard University Press, 1985.

Wertsch, J. V. *Voices of the Mind: A Sociocultural Approach to Mediated Action.* Cambridge: Harvard University Press, 1991.

Whiteley, C. H. *Mind in Action: An Essay in Philosophical Psychology.* London: Oxford University Press, 1973.

Wiener, P. P., ed. *Dictionary of the History of Ideas.* 4 vols. New York: Scribner's, 1973.

Williams, B. *Descartes: The Project of Pure Enquiry.* Atlantic Highlands, NJ: Humanities Press, 1978.

Woolf, L. *Downhill All the Way: An Autobiography of the Years 1919 to 1939.* New York: Harcourt, Brace & World, 1967.

Woolf, L. *The Journey Not the Arrival Matters: An Autobiography of the Years 1939 to 1969.* New York: Harcourt Brace Jovanovich, 1969.

Woolf, V. *The Diary of Virginia Woolf.* Edited by Anne Olivier Bell with Andrew McNeillie. 5 vols. London: Hogarth Press, 1977–1984.

Woolf, V. *The Letters of Virginia Woolf.* Edited by Nigel Nicolson and Joanne Trautmann. 6 vols. London: Hogarth Press, 1975–1980.

Woolf, V. *Moments of Being: Unpublished Autobiographical Writings.* Edited by Jeanne Schulkind. Sussex: The University Press, 1976.

Yapko, M. D. *Suggestions of Abuse: True and False Memories of Childhood Sexual Trauma.* New York: Simon and Schuster, 1994.

Yates, F. A. *The Art of Memory.* Chicago: University of Chicago Press, 1966.

Zivin, G., ed. *The Development of Self-Regulation Through Private Speech.* New York: Wiley, 1979.

Index

About the Author

THOMAS SZASZ, Professor of Psychiatry Emeritus at the State University of New York Health Science Center in Syracuse, New York, is the author of 23 books, among them the classic, *The Myth of Mental Illness* (1961), and *Our Right to Drugs* (Praeger, 1991).